Consciousness-in-Action

Consciousness-in-Action

Toward an Integral Psychology of Liberation & Transformation

Raúl Quiñones Rosado, PhD

ilé Publications
Caguas, Puerto Rico

ilé Publications
ilé, inc.
PMB #117, 200 Ave. Rafael Cordero, Suite 140
Caguas, Puerto Rico 00725
www,conciencia-en-accion.org

Figure on page 28, "Some Examples of the Four Quadrants in Humans" from A THEORY OF EVERYTHING by Ken Wilber
©2000. Reprinted by arrangement with Shambhala Publications,
Inc. Boston, MA, www.shambhala.com

Figures on pages 31-36 from RECREATING THE WORLD: A
PRACTICAL GUIDE TO BUILDING SUSTAINABLE
COMMUNITIES by Michael and Judie Bopp © 2001. Reprinted
with permission from Four Worlds Press, Cochrane, Alberta, Canada

Back cover photo © Jacques-Jean Tiziou / jjtiziou.net

LIBRARY OF CONGRESS CATALOGING-IN-PUBLICATION DATA
Quiñones Rosado, Raúl, 1953—
Consciousness-in-action: toward an integral psychology of libera-
tion & transformation / Raúl Quiñones Rosado.
p. cm.
Includes bibliographical references.
ISBN 978-0-6151-4507-5

To my mother, Tomasa Rosado Soto,
to my father, Fernando Quiñones Allende,
and to my son, Gabriel Hatuey Quiñones Reinat.

To ancestors, *compañeras* and *compañeros*,
and generations to come:
together in spiraling dance toward freedom and love.

Contents

List of Figures

Acknowledgements

Having finally completed this book after many years, I look back, and around me, and see many, many people to whom to give thanks. Indeed, there is an entire community, people with whom I have lived, learned, and struggled as I earned my doctoral degree while also remaining engaged in anti-oppression movements in Vieques, Puerto Rico, and in Latino communities in the US, and while I tried to fulfill my familial responsibilities as partner, father and son.

As this book is based on my doctoral dissertation submitted to and approved by the Graduate College of Union Institute and University, let me begin with my doctoral committee. Each member was very helpful and supportive of my interdisciplinary program of study and unique dissertation proposal since its inception. Adjunct faculty member, Dr. Edwin J. Nichols, provided invaluable guidance and encouragement early on in the conceptualization of the dissertation, and with his vast knowledge of the philosophical aspects of cultural difference served as mentor on issues of race and culture. Dr. Dorothy Firman, my other adjunct faculty member,

consistently encouraged my efforts to explore practical therapeutic applications of my work, and actively supported the
sharing of my views with others in the psychotherapeutic and
academic communities. Peer member Norma Smith, Ph.D.,
was also a steady source of support primarily through her
keen and critical eye, her consistent call for clarity, and her
personal commitment to issues and visions we very much
share. Meanwhile, Aurora Levins Morales, Ph.D., also a peer
member, was a constant source of encouragement and helpful
critique throughout the writing process, and a frequent resource for additional titles and authors worthy of consideration. As a renowned Latina author, Aurora continues to be a
source of inspiration, and has become a dear friend. Core faculty member, Mary T. Sheerin, was just that: a "core" or central figure in the process. Dr. Sheerin's grasp of the scope, in-
tent, and significance of my program generally, my dissertation specifically, and my life-work overall, allowed her to so
skillfully guide me throughout the research and production
phases of my dissertation; her probing, editorial comments,
and encouragement were always welcomed and received as I
fully trusted her genuine interest in my work. Finally, Dr.
Mark Rosenman's review and critique as second core reader
of the dissertation led to a clearer and stronger final product.
To each of them, I will always be deeply appreciative.

So many folks, members of the multiple communities-
of-struggle of which I am a part, influenced this work well
before it was even conceived. My colleagues and friends of
the Latino Empowerment Education study circle—Anna
Mangual Courtier, María Morales Loebl, Ana Rodríguez, and
Carla Classon-Höök—were there with me to prepare the
ground upon which key structures of this framework were
built. Later, work with the hundreds of people that participated in empowerment, leadership development, and organizing efforts of *ilé*, then the Institute for Latino Empowerment,
back when it was still a part of Casa Latina, Inc., motivated

the further elaboration of the model's concepts and liberatory-transformative processes. Many of those early participants, including people like Aixa Quirós, Annie Rodríguez, Paula X. Rojas, Marco Dermith, María Elena Letona, Antonieta Gimeno, Juan Carlos Aguilar, and Amarilis Flores Flores, have gone on to provide integrative and transformative leadership to organizations and anti-oppression community efforts.

Also contributing to the on-going development of the ideas and processes herein are the many people and organizations with whom *ilé* has collaborated and has positively influenced since its establishment in Puerto Rico, among them: Onelia Pérez, Elba Pacheco, and Eulalia Centeno of *Centro Mujer y Nueva Familia*; Judith Conde, Zaida Torres, and the women of the *Alianza de Mujeres Viequenses*; Ismael Guadalupe, Bob Rabin, and Nilda Medina of *Comité Pro Rescate de Vieques*, together with many hundreds of people whom we struggled against the US Navy; as well as the many affiliated with *Alianza Puertorriqueña Antirracista*.

From the very first ten-week workshop offered by *ilé* in the Spring of 1992, Esterla Barreto Cortéz has been a constant presence and positive influence, a force in her own right. Her demand for clarity of thinking, practical, and appropriate application in community, and personal integrity has coincided with—and strengthened—this work. Esterla's early recognition and appreciation of the significance of the principles and practices of the work of consciousness-in-action inspired her to pursue doctoral studies in social policy at Brandeis University; her dissertation was based on participatory action research of the effectiveness of *ilé*'s work toward facilitating a sense of empowerment among its participants. Dr. Barreto Cortéz, who is now associate professor at the Graduate School of Social Work at the University of Puerto Rico, and a founding member of the *Alianza Puertorriqueña Antirracista*, is also currently co-director of *ilé*. I want to thank Esterla very much for helping me over the years to think through and be

clear about many of the ideas and applications of consciousness-in-action. And more to the point of this book, I want to
thank her for being an important outside reader and critic, as
she is perhaps the second most qualified person to evaluate
this work.

I am sure that neither Dr. Barreto Cortéz, nor Drs.
Sheerin, Nichols, Firman, Levins Morales, and Smith, all
whom have met María I. Reinat Pumarejo, will feel in any
way diminished by my claim that she is, indeed, the most
qualified among those who could adequately evaluate this
work. María's qualifications to evaluate the merits of this
work do not stem from her Masters in Education in counseling psychology, or her graduate studies in history of Puerto
Rico, or her many years as Core Trainer with The People's
Institute for Survival & Beyond, or even her nomination for
the 2005 Nobel Peace Prize as one of the 1000 Women for
Peace. In some measure, her qualifications do stem from the
fact that she has been my life partner for the last 15 years, is
the mother of our son, and that we are co-founders, co-
directors, and co-trainer-organizers of *ilé*; as such, she knows
my mind, heart, and behavior better than anyone. But what
truly qualifies María to evaluate this work is the knowledge
and wisdom that stems from her own organizing and leadership development work, her life-long struggle against oppression, and her personal commitment to on-going integral well-
being and growth. Furthermore, as *ilé*'s primary organizer,
María has conceived of, designed, and implemented most of
the organization's integral change strategies presented in the
exemplar section in Chapter 5. Without a doubt, María is the
foremost expert practitioner of integral liberation and transformation I know. For her observations, critiques, questions,
and praises, I thank her. For her emotional support, personal
endurance, and the many sacrifices in our family life through
the long years of study and writing, I thank her. And for being
a constant source of inspiration, thank you, María.

I also want to thank my son, Gabriel Hatuey, for his patience, and for being a constant reminder of the importance of striving toward an integral transformative life. And thanks to my sister, Mabel, and brother, Fernando, for being there in so many ways, most importantly, for sharing the joy and pride that my recent accomplishments represent for our family— especially to our mother and father. I am certain our parents receive in spirit my most deepest love and appreciation for their lives of hard work and sacrifice, for their unwavering commitment to us, for their living example of respect, integrity, and dignity.

Preface

This book is the product of analysis and insight based on years of research and experience that include but extend beyond my program of study as a doctoral learner in the Graduate College of Union Institute and University. While the content of this text is limited to my research, analysis and conceptualization in specific areas within the fields of psychology, sociology, social theory and cultural studies, this book represents but a fragment, albeit an ambitious one, of a much larger work-in-progress, one undertaken in my early adolescence, continued throughout my professional career and, in a more deliberate manner, fully embraced during the past two decades of social change work.

During this time, I have studied and/or worked in such varied fields as psychology, counseling, mental health crisis intervention, housing law, photography, journalism, non-profit management, and organizational development. More recently, my personal and professional life has revolved around anti-oppression work through empowerment education, leadership development, community organizing,

and social action. All the while, I have been engaged in an
on-going study and exploration of spirituality, meditation,
martial arts, and healing arts, through which I have developed
a personal transformative practice.

Together, these experiences have aided my efforts to
understand one of my life's primary concerns: *What is the
root cause of humanity's current state of limited well-being
and development?*

Of course, the question itself presupposes several
"truths" or "realities" and reveals a particular bias or point of
view. For one, it presumes there is such a thing as a scale of
"well-being" that can be "limited," advanced, or even optimal. It also conveys a historic perspective, in that humanity's
"current state" is limited even when at some other time, past
or future, we might (have) enjoy(ed) a different state along
this continuum, hence "development." And as I pose this
question about "humanity's" current state of limited well-
being and development it is clear that I am not just referring
to the people of Puerto Rico, Latinos in the United States, or
the people of the US and its colonies in general. The question
presumes the "currently" "limited" "state" of "well-being"
and "development" of <u>all humankind</u>. Of course, this is a
generalization. I mean it as such. That is to say, while there
may well be exceptions to the rule, my question does presup-
pose that humanity *in general*—individuals, groups, communities, and societies across the planet—does not enjoy a state
of advanced or optimal well-being. Naturally, I intend to define these terms and explain these presuppositions more fully
in the pages that follow.

But the most difficult part of this question for me has
been regarding the notion of "root cause."

For many years, I have affirmed that the root cause of
our current state of limited human well-being and development is **oppression**: the system of differential power that
privileges certain identity groups over, and at the expense of,

others. Initially, I focused my analysis of oppression strictly on race and class, and later on culture and nationality, not surprisingly, identities in which I have subordinated status. Eventually, my awareness of the nature of my own relationship to women and to other men also increased, as did my need to change deeply engrained ideas, beliefs, values, and behaviors regarding issues of gender and sexuality in general. I'm still working at it.

As I gained more awareness of my multiple social identities, both dominant and subordinated, I gained even greater insight. And as I explored internalized superiority and inferiority and how we are all socialized in oppression's insidious ideology, I truly understood that *oppression really does negatively impact us all!* This relationship between institutional oppression and internalized superiority and inferiority, too, is central to what is addressed in this work.

Yet, as I examined and sought to understand oppression as the "root cause of humanity's current state of limited well-being and development," I also wondered: *What is the root cause of oppression?*

This book is part of that on-going exploration. Moreover, this work represents an important personal breakthrough, as I have struggled within a dominant cultural paradigm that insists on linear causality. My "discovery" of an integral perspective, a perspective quite ancient to others, has allowed me to transcend, or "embrace and move beyond" (Wilber, 1999), linear and dichotomous thinking. It is indeed this integral approach that has allowed me to incorporate concepts generally limited to spirituality and consciousness studies, such as the notion of transcendence. However, this integral approach has allowed me to examine human processes at both the individual and collective dimensions of life. It renders both of my "root cause" questions not so much obsolete or irrelevant, as incomplete and limited.

Inevitably, this work is also about my personal quest to make sense of a world that seems to make—or have—none. It is about sharing a map of a territory that has been charted by others before me, but this time drawn as seen through the eyes of this middle-aged, brown-skinned, US-born, Puerto Rico-raised cultural heir to vanquished Taínos, enslaved Africans, and mixed-race Spanish colonizers; this Caribbean, Latin American, and (involuntary) US citizen; this college educated, working class migrant-commuter; Christian, Buddhist, shamanic non-practitioner; partnered heterosexual male and father, who also happens to be an anti-oppression educator, organizer, activist, counselor and, now, social psychologist and scholar.

Like me, this work is a product of a cultural view and a time where the fusion and synthesis of conflicting forces are part of the (un)natural order of the day. It draws from many and varied sources: from social, cognitive, and integral psychologies; from feminism, anti-racism, and other theories of oppression and liberation; from sociology and cultural studies; from consciousness studies and spirituality. Moreover, it draws from life and struggle in community.

So, while my exploration into the systemic or non-linear nature of oppression leads me to the study of development of consciousness, I remain, now more than ever, concerned about the daily lives of people and of our collective future. Now more than ever, I am concerned about life for Latinas/os and other People of Color in towns and cities across the United States. Now more than ever, I am worried about the future of Puerto Ricans here at home, still under colonial rule. Now more than ever, I am worried about oppressed peoples around the world increasingly threatened by the forces of militarism, globalization and cultural imperialism, currently under the guise of anti-terrorism.

That is why now more than ever, I feel within me a sense of great urgency to participate in the development of new knowledge:

- That is useful in disrupting the systemic forces in society that subjugate people everyday.

- That is effective in creating processes that alleviate and transform the devastating effects of oppression in our lives.

- That not only inspires much-needed hope, but also fosters in people a sense of personal and collective power to create life-enhancing alternatives for our communities and ourselves.

- That actually provides people with methods and processes to develop our own local transformative leadership that shall, in turn, help us be self-determining co-creators of our circumstance as a community, as a people.

- That contributes to the development of consciousness into an integral perspective, even if only for small groups of transformative leaders who might in turn influence institutional and cultural transformations.

More than anything else, it is this sense of urgency that motivates me to explore and contribute to the development of an integral psychology of well-being and development that is liberatory and transformative.

Introduction

Out of my life-long concern with personal change and social transformation, I have explored many different approaches to human well-being and development. Throughout,
I have spent time and effort seeking to reconcile what always
appeared to me as, not just major differences, but oppositional stances, between many of these approaches. Even during my earliest days as an undergraduate student in the early
1970s, individual-biased psychology was often pitted against
the "masses" orientation of political science and economics.
Psychology, especially in the eyes of many of my Marxist
contemporaries, had little or nothing to contribute to social
movement. Even prominent figures within the field itself,
such as Franz Fanon (1967) or Thomas Szasz (1960) were
critical of psychology as an instrument of the state designed
to legitimize and maintain an oppressive status quo.

And while this was a view I, for the most part, shared,
I still felt compelled to try to understand individual behavior
and subjectivity, motivated by a belief that this knowledge
could indeed contribute to a better—and freer—society. This

belief was reinforced during a course I took in 1973 in the new field of Humanistic Psychology. Exposure to Maslow (1968, 1971), May (1953), Rogers (1961), Frankl (1963), Jung (1968), Perls (1975), and others strengthened in me both the notion of the potential of the individual *and* of the field of psychology in creating a new world envisioned by a new generation worldwide. What was not yet clear to me was just *how* it could contribute, and moreover, how *I* could be a part of that movement.

As I sought to apply my newly acquired knowledge and insights to the social, political, cultural and economic realities of low-income Puerto Ricans, African-Americans, Southeast Asians, and whites in the US Northeast, my belief in the person-centered approaches of humanistic psychology, or even the broader-but-still-individual orientation of human services, began to waiver. At first, I thought that my lack of success in helping my "clients" reach "their goals" as established in their "individualized service plans" was due to my own lack of experience and skill. I believed I was temporarily experiencing sort of a parallel, albeit, slightly higher-plane version of what my clients had been living—a problem that could easily be solved, by them and by me, with just more knowledge and skills development.

But as the years went by and, in spite of my increased education, experience and skill, there were still no significant changes in the "measurable outcomes" of my clients, or those of colleagues far more experienced. With this, my belief or faith in individual-oriented approaches to employment and training, mental health, educational, or housing virtually vanished. Fortunately, I never got cynical to the point of doing what so many of my colleagues, supervisors, administrators, funders, and, ultimately, the approach itself did: blame the poor—whites and of color alike—for their circumstances and problems. I just knew there was something larger that was responsible, something deeper that was not being acknowledged and addressed.

In reaction to my first taste of what I had labeled as "burn-out," I retreated into a phase of self-examination. This lead me into a deeper exploration of Transcendental Meditation, karate and *taijichuan* (T'ai Chi Chuan), the teachings of Carlos Castañeda (1969, 1972), Gurdjieff and Ouspensky (1957), Taoism (Bynner, 1944), Zen Buddhism (Kapleau, 1980; Suzuki, 1973), guided imagery with music—and back around again to psychology.

This was a most interesting time in the evolution of my thinking about well-being and social change. In the early 1980s, the new field of transpersonal psychology, building upon the contributions of humanistic psychology, was just beginning to emerge. As Maslow, a founder of that movement, looked beyond his hierarchy of needs, he began to explore "the farther reaches of human nature" and aspects of development traditionally only examined by religion and philosophy (Maslow, 1971). Meanwhile, Psychosynthesis, the innovative transpersonal approach to psychotherapy of Roberto Assagioli (1965, 1973) had become relatively well-known and accepted in the United States. Jean Houston (1982) was "midwifing" the human potential movement with her writings, presentations and intensive workshops. Frances Vaughn and Roger Walsh (1980) had just edited a book establishing the field which compiled important contributions by many key theorists of the movement: Maslow, Stanislav Grof, Daniel Goleman, Fritjof Capra, Ram Dass, Charles Tart, Jack Kornfield, Willis Harman, Duane Elgin, James Bugental, and a young Ken Wilber.

What attracted my attention to this new field was its explicit recognition of the spiritual domain as an essential and integral part of human well-being, and its apparent openness to explore beyond European and European-American psychological theory and spiritual traditions. Transpersonal psychology also recognized the body and the notion of optimal physical health as essential to a holistic view of well-being (Houston, 1982). And as the field also began to adopt an ecological view of people and society in relationship to the planet (Elgin, 1980), I felt a sense of hope that psychology was moving beyond its fragmented view of the individual.

All of this coincided with my own independent study and practice in the transpersonal field, primarily through reading of spiritual literature of various traditions, daily practice of meditation, regular practice of *taijichuan*, adopting a lacto-vegetarian diet, counselor training in Psychosynthesis, and participation in Jean Houston's first Mystery School. As I returned to human service work, this study and practice served as a source of physical, emotional, mental, and spiritual sustenance. In time, however, these seemed more like a sanctuary within which I sought to mitigate (escape from?) the impact of the realities of life—of the people with whom I worked as well as my own.

But as I sought transpersonal solutions to everyday problems, ranging from the physical, emotional and sexual abuse of children, to racial discrimination in housing and employment, lack of access to health and human services, to the systematic expulsion of Latino/a children from public schools, my old internal conflict between "help-the-individual" versus "change-the-system" approaches resurfaced with a vengeance. Of course, it did not help much that most of my friends, colleagues, and teachers seemed essentially unaware of, or basically unconcerned with, racist, classist, or eurocentrist oppression.

This was particularly frustrating given that many of the people with whom I worked and interacted were very much aware of and concerned with sexism, homophobia, and/or the need for multicultural education. Some were also quite concerned with apartheid in South Africa and civil wars in Central America; a few of them actively opposed racism and US imperialism abroad. However, I was always amazed at how some of these very same people could be so blind to the struggles of the women, men, children, and elders of the Puerto Rican and African American communities living right there in the cities and towns of greater Springfield, Massachusetts, right there in their own backyards. While many seemed to intellectually grasp racism and classism almost as well as they grasped sexism, heterosexism, and imperialism, somehow they seemed unable, or unwilling, to reckon with the very real impact of these particular forms of oppression. Not surprisingly, I suspected they were simply unable or unwilling to confront themselves with their own participation in this social dynamic.

Meanwhile, the pendular swing of my own renewed existential crisis landed me once again on the "change the system" side of this conflict of opposites. But this time, instead of retreating into my head and body out of the frustration and pain in my heart and soul, I knew it was time to take action. I knew it was time to actually try my hand at doing something about changing conditions that negatively affected people in my own community of struggle.

By 1988, when I accepted the position of executive director of Casa Latina, Inc., a Latino community organization in western Massachusetts, I had no illusions of "saving the world" or "changing the system," or even of "taking on City Hall." I just had a sense that I had to step up and step in with creative energy and try something different. Well, "the system" lost no time in letting me know what the impact of an economic downturn can be on small community nonprofit, never mind on the marginalized communities themselves. Not six months into the job, Casa Latina had lost half its budget and more than half its miniscule staff due to federal, state and municipal government cutbacks of social service funding. The next two years were spent dealing on a

week-to-week basis with the fiscal survival of this 25 year-
old organization.

To me, the problem was more than securing funding
for staff and services. There were other larger, albeit white-
led, organizations eager for a "merger" with Casa Latina; being able to claim to directly serve the county's largest community of color would have gone a long way to secure and
expand additional (and desperately needed) funds, while cost-
ing the "umbrella" or "parent" organization only one, maybe
two, seats on their otherwise all-white Boards of Directors.
For me, and for the board of Casa Latina, the issue was
whether our community was able to sustain, lead, and guide
an organization in accordance with its own needs and cultur-
ally-based vision. It was a matter of community empowerment and self-determination.

A series of events, the multitude of issues, and the
complexity of the dynamics of this period (from 1988
through 1996), particularly in the context of my leadership
role within the organization and the community, was crucial
to the development of an integral perspective. Added to my
previous fourteen years in human services, these experiences
led me to re-examine and re-evaluate my understanding of
the organization and its history, its role and purpose, its relationship to the Latino community and to the community at
large, and to its effectiveness toward improving conditions
for Latinos/as. Moreover, this review of our organization and
community led me to a critical analysis of the larger system.

Of special significance were the work sessions of the
Latino Empowerment Study Circle, a small group of Latino/a
colleagues that gathered almost weekly for two years to seriously pursue this in-depth analysis. I remember we started
out by asking ourselves questions such as: "How is it that after twenty-five years of providing English-as-a-Second-
Language classes, employment counseling, information and
referral services, health education, cultural events, recrea-

tional activities, economic development opportunities, and advocacy, the overall situation of Latinos/as in our cities is worse now than when our organizations were founded? What are the <u>real</u> problems of our community anyway? What are the <u>root causes</u> of these problems? Do our organizations and their many "programs" even address these root causes? Are our members—staff, board members, participants, and community constituents in general—even aware of these root causes? And if we do not address these root causes, what impact can we expect to have on actually <u>changing</u> the social, political, cultural, and economic conditions that give rise to the specific problems of our communities and their individual members?"

Now, each one of us in the group certainly knew about the impact of racism, classism, sexism, and other forms of oppression, mostly from our very own life experiences, but also from various college courses, workshops and professional training we had taken over the years. But to do an honest and open critical analysis of our own organizations in the context of institutional oppression was something none of us had ever done. Yet, none of us was surprised by our conclusions. We were, however, more than a bit overwhelmed. I certainly was. I mean, it was one thing to want to contribute and create positive change at a level beyond the individual, and it is quite another to really "take on the system"—the institutions and the underlying culture of oppression itself. Besides, where does one begin? *Where* is "the system" and *who* is it, anyway? Aren't we Latinos/as part of the system? Shouldn't we start there? Do we focus on racism only? But, isn't racism intricately linked to classism and eurocentrism anyway? How do we deal with colorism among Latinos/as and our learned negative biases toward African Americans and other People of Color, even toward Latinos/as of other nationalities? What about sexism within our own community and culture? But doesn't focusing on "the victims of oppression" border on blaming them and, meanwhile, letting "the oppressors" off the hook? Though, if there are multiple oppressions going on simultaneously, with everyone being impacted in some way or fashion, who, then, is "victim" and who is "oppressor"? How can we even begin to get a handle on all these complex issues, not to mention the many and often conflicting feelings they inevitably arouse?

My mind-mapped notes and diagrams seemed more complex and intertwined than the new neural pathways surely being activated in my severely overloaded neo-cortex. Confusion and, moreover, despair could have easily been the main outcome of these regular and very intense meetings, especially had we engaged in the dichotomous-thinking, debate-driven style of inquiry in which we had all been well trained. Instead, early on we chose to honor our shared cultural inclination to express our fears, frustrations, hunches, hopes and humor at least as often as our reasoned observations and seasoned analytical prowess.

It was during one of our early meetings that my dear friend and colleague, María Morales, MPH, a Chicana from New Mexico and executive director of Spanish American Union (Casa Hispana), introduced us to a model of well-being to which she had recently been exposed. Exposure to the concepts and principles of the Lakota medicine wheel created a fundamental shift in my conception of well-being and development, and in doing so, resolved for me the basis of my professional, intellectual, even existential, dilemma of having to choose between individual- or collective-level approaches. The circular configuration of this indigenous integral view (J. Bopp, Michael Bopp, Lee Brown, and Phil Lane, Jr., 1984/1989) broke the dualistic patterns characteristic of European thought (Ani, 1994) to which I was so accustomed, given the colonizing nature of my education.

As an organizational manager, planner, program designer, fundraiser, grantwriter, spokesperson and leader, and later as workshop facilitator, Latino leadership trainer, and community organizer, I found that the Lakota medicine wheel, as presented by the Four Worlds Development Project (Bopp et al., 1984), offered a very simple and practical tool that could be easily used by people in our communities, regardless of their level of schooling, to begin to critically analyze disruptors of well-being. This new approach, naturally, could (and would) be used to open new pathways to generate shared holistic visions toward more integral solutions to the problems confronted by oppressed communities.

As a social scientist in-the-field, I found the integral Lakota model offered a unified view of aspects of the person (e.g., physical, mental, spiritual and emotional) and society (e.g., economic, political, cultural and social) that in academia are studied in fragmented fashion as if these aspects were discrete and isolated from one another. The more I considered and examined this seemingly simple model, the more I discovered how well it served as a framework upon which I could continue to build. As I had already begun to do, the medicine wheel's foundation would allow me to integrate many other important concepts and principles of psychology, spirituality, and critical theory I had found useful along the way.

My integration of this knowledge and this perspective inspired a two-fold pursuit. First, it inspired the founding of ilé: Institute for Latino Empowerment as a vehicle for Latino leadership development, an organization I co-directed from 1992 to 2005, and through which I also trained and organized. Secondly, this transformative process also inspired the on-going development of unique conceptual synthesis and its application in an innovative anti-oppression education and organizing approach. With it began a period of intense creativity and community engagement, and eventually, the decision to pursue doctoral studies and undertake the research that further informs this book.

The driving force of this pursuit, however, goes well beyond my own personal need to resolve existential conflicts, philosophical incongruities, organizational concerns, or even the problems of a particular community. The motivation comes from having observed a persistent pattern of fragmentation of perspective, of analysis, and of action—even among people who are undoubtedly aware of and wholeheartedly committed to positive social change.

Throughout my involvement in social movements and participation in specific anti-oppression struggles in Puerto Rico and the US during the last fifteen years, I have witnessed how the lack of a broad, system-of-systems perspective with a unifying conceptual framework has kept progressive people and organizations divided among each other and, in large measure, separated from the very communities they seek to liberate. I have witnessed brilliant anti-oppression leaders rendered ineffective by their inability to manage the stresses inherent in their work or, worse, by their lack of emotional intelligence in the face of their own oppressive attitudes, beliefs, and behaviors in social contexts in which they enjoy dominant status. To this day, I continue to witness how precious opportunities for the advancement of liberation struggles are squandered, not only because of very powerful institutional forces determined to maintain their privileged status, but also by people within the movement itself.

In my view, this tendency toward fragmentation and separation is indeed one of society's most crucial problems, perhaps even the most central "meta-problem" of our times. The fragmented and fragmenting approaches generated by this prevailing tendency are problems that could be addressed with the adoption of integral perspectives that allow for integral analyses that, in turn, could give rise to the formulation of integral and unifying strategies leading to eventual larger scale social transformations.

As I attempt to move beyond fragmented perspectives and approaches to well-being and social change based on compartmentalized views and narrow analyses, through this work I seek to address a most critical question:

> *What would a comprehensive and cohesive conceptual framework of human well-being in the context of institutional and internalized oppression look like, one that takes into account multiple perspectives, and that views well-being as a process of liberation from oppression and development as transformation at both individual and collective dimensions of life?*

In an effort to address this question, this book presents an integral framework of well-being and development. This framework is based on theories from psychology, sociology, critical theory, and cultural studies, and is further informed by my experience as a community educator and organizer, leadership development trainer, program and curriculum designer, psycho-educational counselor, spiritual and healing arts practitioner, and political activist.

This framework joins the holistic perspectives of the Lakota medicine wheel (Bopp et al., 1989; Bopp, Bopp, and Lane, 1998; M. Bopp and J. Bopp, 2001), and integral psychology (Wilber, 1999b). It considers the spectrum of human development inclusive of the mental, emotional, physical, and spiritual aspects some of which are typically neglected by traditional psychology, or even by the fields of critical and community psychology (Fox and Prilleltensky, 1997; Nelson and Prilleltensky, 2005). While integral psychology as of late has begun to acknowledge the social and cultural contexts in which human development unfolds, this approach remains primarily individualistic and essentially Eurocentric despite its references to, if not misappropriations of, Asian and Native cultures; it appears to both minimize the significance of the social construction of race, gender, class, and other group identities, and virtually ignores the dynamics of institutional power as a critically important force in the process of individual growth and social evolution.

At the same time, this work has much in common with the fields of social and community psychology, as these are very much concerned with issues of power and oppression and view individuals within from their collective sociopolitical context. I am particularly interested in the foundational thought of Frantz Fanon (1963, 1976; Bulhan, 1985), Paulo Freire (Collins, 1977; Freire, 1970; Horton, 1990; McLaren and Leonard, 1993), Ignacio Martín-Baró (1989, 1994), Maritza Montero (1994, 1997, 2003, 2004, 1987, 1991), bell hooks (1993, 1995, 2000a, 2000b), Na'im Akbar (1984, 1996), and others in what is often referred to as psychology of oppression and liberation. Their works have emerged out of the struggles of People of Color to survive and thrive in the face of racial, colonial, class and gender oppression; their works reflect human attempts to understand our own psyche and our will—individually and collectively—to overcome the dehumanizing conditions historically imposed upon oppressed peoples.

This comprehensive and cohesive theoretical framework seeks to describe the structures and processes inherent to human well-being and development from an integral perspective that is both liberatory and transformative. A contribution to both integral and social psychologies, this book presents a framework comprised of four basic components:

- A model of the aspects, dimensions, and key elements of integral well-being and development, and the dynamic relationship between these components.
- An analysis of social forces that hinder integral well-being and development.
- A description of the process of "consciousness-in-action" toward liberation in the context of institutional and internalized oppression.

- A proposed integral approach to change that is both liberatory and transformative, and that is simultaneously oriented to both personal and collective dimensions.

Chapter 1: Toward an Integral View begins by framing the need for an integral approach to well-being from the perspective of a "scholar-practitioner" whose primary concern is creating positive change in community and, ultimately, transforming society. Definitions for the key concepts *integral*, *well-being*, and *development* are elaborated throughout the chapter. In so doing, I discuss foundational concepts and principles of the Medicine Wheel model as presented by The Four Worlds Development Project (Bopp et al., 1989; Bopp et al., 1998; Bopp and Bopp, 2001) and of Wilber's integral theory (1996, 1997, 1998, 1999b, 1999c, 1999d, 1999e, 2000a, 2000c, 2000d, 2002, 2003a, 2003b).

In *Chapter 2: Reworking the Frame*, I introduce an approach to integral well-being (Quiñones Rosado and Barreto-Cortéz, 2000, 2002), inspired by the Lakota medicine wheel model and consistent with integral theory. This adaptation includes concepts from a wide range of sources, which include Psychosynthesis (Assagioli, 1965/1976, 1973; Brown, 1983; Ferrucci, 1982; Firman and Gila, 1997, 2002), vipassana meditation (Goenka, 1987; Hart, 1987), and liberation pedagogy (Freire, 1970; Hope and Timmel, 1984), among other influences. Supported by original figures to illustrate the basic structures of the self in society, the model maps out the different aspects, elements and functions in the individual and collective dimensions of life. Here, I extend this basic framework to include social group identities (Hardiman and Jackson, 1997; Jackson, 2001; Wijeyesinghe and Jackson, 2001) as they are essential aspects of the self and key to an integral view of well-being and development. Moreover, in describing the processes inherent in human well-being and development, this model emphasizes the dynamic and interdependent nature of the relationships between all of the aspects, elements, and functions within and across both individual and collective dimensions.

Building upon this framework, in *Chapter 3: The Forces That Hinder*, I incorporate an analysis of the social, cultural, economic and political forces generated by institutional (structural) oppression and the impact of these forces on people subordinated by virtue of their social group memberships. More specifically, this analysis examines the dynamics of racism, ethnocentrism, colonialism, classism, sexism, and heterosexism, and the effects of the internalization of these forms of oppression in the context of the US and its colony, Puerto Rico—the two contexts in which this analysis, through research and praxis, has been developed. Here, I pay special attention to the psychosocial aspects of oppression, and describe manifestations of internalized inferiority: the negative and self-limiting ideas, feelings, beliefs, behaviors and values with which subordinated people are socialized, and which they come to adopt as their own. Jackson and Hardiman's (1997) social group identity development theory provides a very useful model of the various developmental stages, which is compatible with other processes presented.

In *Chapter 4: Consciousness-in-Action*, I go on to offer a description of conscientization (Freire, 1970), or consciousness-in-action (Quiñones Rosado and Barreto-Cortéz, 2002), as a socio-cognitive-emotional process of perceiving, recognizing, understanding and responding to internalized oppression through the stages of social identity development. This process of consciousness-in-action, I suggest, is essential to liberation and transformation. This is where liberation theory and integral theory unwittingly meet. Aiding the process (or perhaps mediating the clash) are approaches from other unlikely sources, including neurolinguistic psychology (Bandler, 1985, 1992a, 1992b, 1993; Bandler and Mac-

Donald, 1988; Bodenhamer and Hall, 2000; Dilts, 1987, 1990, 1996, 1998) and spiritual practice (Adair, 2001, 2003; Goenka, 1987; Hart, 1987; Walsh, 1999).

In *Chapter 5: An Approach to Integral Change*, I conclude this book by proposing an integral practice that simultaneously supports personal and social processes of liberation and transformation. Recognizing the complementarities of these two processes, I describe liberation as essentially remedial, primarily about resisting, undoing, and overcoming oppression while healing or repairing the harm caused by it. Meanwhile, I describe transformation as generative, about creating change on the basis of more inclusive perspectives and worldviews, deeper understanding and respect, shared values and vision, and the development of new and responsive behavior patterns. Both liberation and transformation are necessary forces for positive change in self and others toward integral change.

Not having encountered exemplars of integral liberatory-transformative approach in the fullest sense (a standard which may very well be impossible to meet), I instead share examples of efforts that, intentionally or unwittingly, approximate an integral orientation to personal change and social transformation.

This book puts forth an original conceptual-pragmatic model conceived, researched, and developed in the context of praxis in community. With this framework, I hope to contribute an integral approach to change that has been missing from liberation psychology while simultaneously bringing an anti-oppression and liberatory perspective that is largely absent in integral psychology. Toward that end, this theoretical framework may serve as the basis for an integral psychology of liberation and transformation.

More specifically, I hope my work will contribute to scholarship and community praxis by:

- offering an expanded, contextually-focused, socio-political-economic-cultural, alternative perspective to the constricted, fixed-focused, individual-centered perspective of psychology and related fields.
- offering a broader biological-mental-emotional-spiritual worldview as an alternative to the narrower psychosocial perspective of social and community psychologies and related fields.
- providing an anti-oppression perspective to the fields of integral psychology, cognitive psychology, social psychology, and related fields.
- addressing the need for deep personal change for social transformation workers and leaders, and offering an integral framework upon which such change processes may be created at the individual dimension (mental, spiritual, emotional, physical), and at the collective dimension (political, cultural, social, economic).

This work is directed at two important audiences: (1) people committed to and actively engaged in organizing against oppression in its many forms, and (2) practitioners and scholars in the fields of psychology, sociology, social work, multicultural organizational development, community development and planning, and public policy. Academics in community, critical or radical psychology may find it a useful contribution, as it seeks to expand their "depth of field" by inserting both psycho-spiritual perspectives and cognitive approaches to socio-political concerns. Similarly, this work may well be relevant to therapists, counselors, community workers, and other helping professionals working with and within communities of struggle.

As practitioners and thinkers in transpersonal and integral psychology become more interested in the key social, political, and culture issues of our day, they too may find this work useful. They will find that it expands the notion of "integral" or "holistic," concepts central to those fields, to include the collective dimension of human experience. Furthermore, they will discover the importance of addressing institutional power and social dynamics, and their impact upon our psycho-spiritual development, as essential issues in any serious discussion of well-being.

I anticipate that this work will be of special interest to Puerto Ricans and other Latinas/os, given that it frequently references experiences in my own community, experiences that are commonly shared regarding issues and circumstances to which many Latinos/as can relate. And to the extent that these circumstances, issues and experiences are also shared by other oppressed communities, this work may very well be of interest to other People of Color, women, poor and working class folks, gay, lesbian, bisexual, and transgendered persons, and others subordinated by virtue of their culture, nationality, religion, age or other social group membership. Hopefully, we will be reminded that the key concepts, principles, and processes involving internalized oppression are similar for all oppressed peoples.

And since one of the premises of this work is that everyone is negatively impacted by oppression, this work may also be found useful to whites, men, owning class members, heterosexuals, people of European descent, Christians, and all who, by virtue of their membership in key social groups, collectively wield power over the lives of others.

Most importantly, this work is directed at anyone actively engaged in struggles against racism, ethnocentrism, colonialism, classism, sexism, heterosexism, and other forms of oppression; it is for everyone seriously committed to liberating and transforming their own lives, their own communities, their own societies — our own world.

Chapter 1

Toward an Integral View

To understand the whole, it is necessary to understand the parts. To understand the parts, it is necessary to understand the whole. Such is the circle of understanding.

We move from part to whole and back again, and in that dance of comprehension, in that amazing circle of understanding, we come alive to meaning, to value, and to vision: the very circle of understanding guides our way, weaving together the pieces, healing the fractures, mending the torn and tortured fragments, lighting the way ahead—this extraordinary movement from part to whole and back again, with healing the hallmark of each and every step, and grace the tender reward.

Ken Wilber
The Eye of Spirit:
An Integral Vision of a World Gone Slightly Mad
(1998, p. 1)

In my search of a viable alternative to the fragmented and "tortured" approaches encountered in both human development theory and personal and social change practice, two sources have provided a solid foundation of knowledge and wisdom, if not inspiration. One source has been the encyclopedic work of psychological theorist and philosopher Ken Wilber, a major influence on my thinking since 1980, when I first read *The Spectrum of Consciousness* (1977), a seminal work of transpersonal psychology. His integral theory (Wilber, 1996, 1997, 1998, 1999d, 1999e, 2000a, 2000d), and more specifically, his integral psychology (Wilber, 1999b, 1999e, 2000c), which embraces yet transcends the transpersonal approach (Tart, 1992; Walsh and Vaughn, 1980; Welwood, 2000; Wilber, 1977, 1980, 1981), continues to deepen my understanding, particularly as it explores and proposes

the on-going elaboration of an *integral* or "inclusive, balanced, comprehensive" (Wilber, 2003b, p. 1) model of human development.

The other major source of knowledge and inspiration,
rooted in tribal wisdom, harvested from community action in
Canada, and related to similar thought systems in indigenous
communities throughout the world, has been the medicine
wheel model as presented by Four Worlds Development Project (Bopp, et al., 1989; Bopp, et al., 1998; Bopp and Bopp,
2001). Brought to my attention nearly ten years before my re-
encounter with Wilber and his emerging integral theory, this
medicine wheel model was what guided my entry into an integral perspective, providing me with a conceptual framework to understanding the interrelatedness of problems in
community, and equipping me with a functional framework
from which to develop life-enhancing approaches to these
problems.

The purpose of this chapter is to provide a conceptual
context concerning the integral orientation of my work. To
that end, in this chapter I briefly introduce key aspects of
both Wilber's integral theory and the Four Worlds' medicine
wheel model. Precisely because both models are comprehensive in their scope and depth, it would be impractical (if not
impossible) to (re)present them here fully. Therefore, I have
limited this presentation to those concepts and principles
concerning integral well-being and development, as these are
most relevant to my own framework in the chapters that follow. These key concepts, and those from other important influences, will be further elaborated throughout the text as
necessary.

However, before proceeding with this presentation, I
feel it necessary to further contextualize these models with
some of my observations as an organizer regarding the problem of fragmentation.

The Need to Move Beyond Fragmentation

In some ways, a community organizer's work seems rather straight-forward: you work where the problem is at, that issue upon which people in a given community are placing their attention, which, usually, is where they are hurting the most at that particular time. After all, folks generally don't set aside time from their busy and difficult lives to come together just to talk about things unless these are urgent and result in some degree of pain. People in community certainly just do not tend to come together to talk about, much less theorize about, integral well-being and development. They already know they are not "being" all too well, nor perceive they are "developing" all that very much. When community folks attend an organizing meeting or to take part in an empowerment workshop, they usually come to address very specific problems and to see what other people are doing, or are going to do, to deal with these.

Not that organizers, educators, activists, social workers, cultural workers, helping professionals and others committed to social transformation spend a whole lot of time talking and theorizing about well-being and development, either. We usually already have our own analyses of why people are oppressed, and have our own sense of how we would like the world to be. We hold onto these beliefs and visions, even if it has been quite some time since we last got together with colleagues and community to check if our thinking and vision still hold up, or if they are still actually shared among the group. As members of groups and communities-of-struggle (Saldaña-Portillo, 2002) that are oppressed (as we are often from the very same groups and communities in which we organize), we, too, tend to focus our energies and efforts on developing strategies for change, on implementing tactics that will somehow force the institutional powers-that-be into at least some positive reaction. Time for reflection almost seems like a luxury we cannot afford.

I know that in my experience, when asked to describe the circumstances and conditions of their lives, people who live, work and struggle in community quite quickly generate a long list of problems: poverty, unemployment and under-employment; lack of adequate housing, education, recreation and health care; crime and violence; police harassment and brutality; workplace discrimination; government inaction and political corruption; mental illness, alcoholism, and drug addiction; child abuse and neglect; violence against women... Even those of us in groups, organizations and institutions allegedly designed to address these issues readily identify (and invariably complain about) the lack of human and financial resources, inadequate education and training, overwhelming work conditions and unreasonable expectations, turf wars and bureaucracy, big egos and petty politics. Not surprisingly, we, too, often suffer from depression, despair, and a sense of hopelessness in both our professional and personal lives. Seldom do we talk about integral well-being and development for ourselves, much less for the folks with and for whom we work. The problems we encounter daily are simply too many, too serious, too urgent to be considering such matters. We want solutions, even if only temporary and superficial. We want the "band-aid," the "quick fix" — and we want it NOW!

Certainly there are plenty of organizers, activists, teachers, service providers, policy makers, as well as good plain old community folk (in some cases, they are one and the same), that do have a historical perspective and political analysis of these problems and issues. And even if they don't have it clearly articulated or thought out, when asked to explain just why these problems exist and persist, it usually doesn't take long for them to conclude that there are forces—social, political, economic and cultural—that negatively impact their lives. It does not take long at all for people who work in community to name racism, classism, sexism, and other forms of oppression as the root causes of these serious and chronic problems.

Fortunately for social movement, some folks upon reaching this conclusion do become engaged in struggle against oppression, or at least get involved in actions against the form of oppression that most directly and immediately negatively impacts their lives, given their most salient social group identity at the time. Sometimes, though, it seems that people in movements for social change are more clearly *against* something than *for* something, except perhaps as being *for* a society free of racist, sexist, capitalist oppression, which doesn't necessarily offer much by way of a specific direction for movement, a clear vision of new society or new social order. It remains basically reactive.

Of course, there are those proponents of a social order that would merely reverse the roles of dominants and subordinated groups in today's oppressive society, leaving its oppressive nature intact. It makes me recall one of the many chants of the Puerto Rican left during the late 1960s and '70s: *"¡Arriba los de abajo!"* ("Up with the downtrodden!"), the campaign slogan of the pro-independence *Partido Independentista Puertorriqueño*. Not quite as radical as it may have seemed, considering that it was still merely reactive, this clamor for freedom proposed no fundamental (foundational) change in the dynamics of power.

In both Puerto Rico and the United States, most social change efforts or movements seem very fragmented. In Puerto Rico, for example, while there are many efforts aimed at alleviating the symptoms, or even the causes, of social injustice, most groups do not share a comprehensive or integral analysis of the dynamics of oppression and its different manifestations. The anti-militarism movement, for instance, while steeped in an analysis of colonialism, tends to falter in understanding its connection to struggles against racism and eurocentrism; sexism and homophobia goes virtually unexamined, as women (regardless of their sexuality) and men known or suspected to be gay or bi-sexual are so often relegated to lesser roles, if not excluded altogether, their capacity for leadership left untapped.

Meanwhile, approaches to addressing gendered violence tend to be centered on service delivery to women, to the neglect of empowerment and community organizing strategies. These assistentialist approaches are often mandated by assimilationist colonial government policies modeled after intervention efforts in the US, especially in the absence of an indigenous family-centric, anti-racist, Puerto Rican feminist model of intervention. Furthermore, issues of class, education, and geography tend to limit the broad participation of women, while men are virtually absent from the struggle against sexist oppression. Organizing to create institutional change, or to shift culturally pervasive sexist attitudes regarding violence against women by men, is minimal.

Racism as an organizing issue is almost totally overlooked by all, as it is most often mistaken for, if not dismissed as, classism. This ignores the reality that the ideology of white superiority—inherited by Puerto Ricans from Spain, and reinforced by last 109 years of US imperialism—exists even here among a *mestizo-mulato* population that historically has been virtually totally racially mixed (Buscaglia-Salgado, 2003; Comas-Díaz, 1996; Rivera Ramos, 2001). In fact, issues of racial identity and power inequity by race in Puerto Rico are denied to such extreme that in the US Census 2000, 80% of the population here claimed to be white! (Bureau of the Census, 2001)

Not surprisingly, our issues of racial identity in the US are not all that different. And not only among Puerto Ricans, but among Chicanos, Mexicans, Dominicans, Cubans, Hondurans, Salvadorans, Guatemalans, Panamanians and other Latinos/as, as almost half of Latinos/as and Latin American immigrants claim to be white (Bureau of the Census, 2001). Because of our confusion about race and racism in the US, we each struggle separately and on too many fronts. Our differences on the basis of national identity, US citizenship, cultural idiosyncrasies, time in the US, and degree of integration or assimilation, are also very important factors that foster fragmentation (Ferdman, 2001; Quiñones Rosado, 1998; Rodríguez, 2000; Suro, 2002).

Though apparently clearer on the meaning of race and the impact of racism in the US than Latinas/os, it seems to me that African-Americans as a community of struggle are also fragmented in many ways, especially around issues of class. Yet given the national and cultural identity born from the African-*American* experience in the United States, there is a sense of difference and separation between and among US Blacks and other more recent members of the African diaspora in the States—from Puerto Rico and other parts of the Caribbean and South America, and from the African continent itself.

Like racial and national identity, culture and history are also factors that give rise to fragmentation and lack of unity among other communities of color in the US. This is certainly the case with First Nation people. While it may be convenient, even to those of us doing anti-racism work, to think of Native Americans as a group, there are indeed hundreds of tribal communities with their own distinct identities. It is easy, moreover, to refer to "the Asian-American community," yet there really is no such "community." This is not surprising given that the groups that comprise this racial category include, among others, Chinese, Japanese, Korean, Vietnamese, Laotian, Cambodian, Philippino, other Pacific Islanders, Indian, Pakistani—many of whom have long, long histories of animosity and war between and among one another, not to mention other significant cultural differences of language, religion, foods and traditions.

Fragmentation is also a reality within the women's movement: around class lines, racial lines, sexual orientation, nationality, degree of political radicalism (Hill Collins, 2000; Hurtado, 1996; Mohanty, 2003).

And if there is fragmentation within communities of struggle, there is certainly fragmentation between struggles. Naturally, each group believes its perspective and analysis is the correct one, e.g., that sexism is learned before any other form of oppression and therefore should be dealt with first; or that racism is what keeps all groups from being able to work together; or that both sexism and racism are really only manifestations of capitalism, used as a tool to divide and conquer, and therefore, the true culprit and ultimate cause of human suffering. Each of these arguments I have encountered countless times among very committed organizers and social change workers.

As if these sociological and ideological fragmentations were not enough, there is also fragmentation in the many approaches to addressing the process of change and transformation. If you believe that social change is achieved by changing individuals, then the approach tends to be educational, psychological, or perhaps even spiritual, focused on the individual as the basic unit of society. Perhaps your experience informs you of the importance of family and community as support systems in change strategies, and you adopt a more social work or social psychology approach.

Maybe, though, you are convinced that the entire system must be changed, including the educational system, the economic system, the political and judicial system, organized religion, the mass media, and the other institutions that comprise and control our way of life. Therefore, then perhaps your approach is anywhere from political campaigning and lobbying (top down), to mass mobilizations and community organizing (bottom up), to organizational development (inside out).

In societies where fragmentation, separation, and specialization are defining characteristics of the prevailing cultural paradigms, as in Puerto Rico and the US, it is not surprising that even social movements themselves would also be fragmented.

However, the fact that there are so many divisions among communities of struggle, each with its own agenda and preferred ideology, analysis, or methodology for change, is not the biggest problem. To me, the biggest problem is that, by not being able to see the broader picture and how all struggles are interrelated, people in social movements do not seem to be able to come together to effectively organize against oppression and for fundamental social change. Moreover, given the personal sacrifices and risks involved, it is not as if there is currently a large percentage of the population actively engaged in organized social change efforts. Therefore, for those of us in social movement the niche marketing of highly differentiated approaches to liberation is not exactly a promising strategy.

Yet while recognizing that people and communities do tend to come together around specific issues to search for specific solutions they perceive as impacting their lives specifically, I believe an integral—and integrating—view can benefit both specific single-issue groups and the larger movement by providing an orientating frame of the whole. Both Wilber's integral theory and the Four Worlds' medicine wheel model have provided such an effective orientation to my own vision of an integral liberation framework. Here is an introduction to those concepts that inform and shape the work that follows.

Wilber's Integral Approach

Wilber's integral theory is a "comprehensive map of human capacities" resulting from an extensive "cross-cultural comparison of most of the known forms of human inquiry"

(Wilber, 2003b), among which are the fields of psychology, sociology, cultural studies, politics, philosophy, spirituality, and science.

Integral psychology, contained within this overarching theory, seeks to integrate knowledge from psychoanalysis, behaviorism, cognitive, humanistic, and transpersonal psychologies into a coherent and unified—and unifying—theory. Wilber, himself, establishes the basic structures for the correlations between these theories, and makes specific contributions to almost each area researched.

As a comprehensive, non-reductionistic approach, integral psychology is concerned with the evolution of human consciousness. According to Wilber (1999b), this evolution results from development along four central aspects: *lines* of development; *levels* (or stages) of development; *states* of consciousness; and; *the self* or self-system.

Lines of development refer to the multiple human capacities, intelligences, and functions including cognitive aspects and worldviews, as well as ego development, self-identity, moral judgment, affect, needs, spirituality, and numerous others. In the source text, *Integral Psychology* (1999b), Wilber charts out correlations between multiple aspects of approximately one hundred psychological, sociocultural, and spiritual developmental theories, among these: Aurobindo (psycho-spiritual); Cook-Greuter (self-related stages); Erikson (identity); Gebser (sociocultural); Gilligan (feminist perspective on moral stages); Graves (ego types); Habermas (ethics, identity); Kegan (self); Kohlberg (moral judgment); Lenski (techno-economic); Loevinger (ego); Maslow (needs); Piaget (cognitive); Theresa of Ávila (interior life).

Levels refer to milestones or stages of growth and development throughout life across the various lines of development. These lines unfold through the levels, asymmetrically, each at a different rate and, to some extent independent of other lines; they seem to evolve in response to specific tasks (cognitive, linguistic, moral, etc.) within environmental, cultural, and social contexts. For example, someone can be functional at a formal operational cognitive development stage, yet be dealing with issues at the basic safety or belonging needs development stage, while at an egocentric stage of consciousness development (Wilber, 1999b, 2000c). A level or stage of development is attained when the traits that characterize it are permanently integrated. However, as Wilber (1999b, 2000c) explains, levels or stages are not like rungs on a ladder, where to reach the next one you leave the last one behind. Rather, one transcends, or moves beyond a given stage while enfolding and including the tasks and traits of the preceding stages in any given line of development.

Typically, psychology is concerned with normal or ordinary *states of consciousness*: waking, dreaming, and deep sleep. In integral psychology, altered or non-ordinary states of consciousness are also acknowledged and addressed, states often referred to as peak experiences, religious experiences, drug states, and meditative or contemplative states. These altered states can be accessed or experienced by anyone at any stage or level of development, evidence of the non-linear nature of human consciousness development (Wilber, 2000c).

The fourth central aspect considered by integral psychology is *the self*. Wilber refers to the self as "that which attempts to integrate or balance all of the components of the psyche" (2000c, p. 4), namely, the different states of consciousness, multiple lines of development, and their various stages. As a functional system, the self (or self-system) also has the capacity to differentiate, will, defend itself, and regulate tension. Among the defining characteristics of the self is its ability and tendency to *identify* with the basic structures, patterns, or contents of consciousness. In doing so, it generates specific types of self-identity (ibid).

Described another way, because of the self's ability to be aware of itself (self-reflexiveness), I am not only aware of myself, but I *can* and *tend to* identify with aspects (both objective and subjective) of myself (or, rather, this consciousness or field of awareness with which this particular body is associated). Therefore, in my own case, because this center of conscious awareness has become subjectively associated with a body, sensations, perceptions, emotional states, thoughts, memories, imaginations, personal traits, social roles and relationships—all at various stages along the multiple lines of development—I sense, feel, and think my *self* to be, and thus, I tend to say: "I am Raúl," "I am a man," "I am intelligent," "...Latino," "...excited," "...a father," "...a good person," "...healthy," "...a spiritually evolved soul," and so on.

Wilber goes on to explain that individual development, then, is the process by which the self successfully negotiates a *fulcrum* of self-development, the point or juncture where the self encounters a new developmental level (or stage) of consciousness along a particular developmental line. In this process, the self identifies and becomes fused with a new level, then eventually disidentifies with, or transcends, that level as it begins to identify with the next level, ideally integrating the preceding level and the new one. When this process of fusion, transcendence, and integration fails then, claims Wilber, is when most psychopathologies develop (2000).

Most of the examples provided so far describe development of the levels, lines, states, and the self system from the perspective of the interior (or subjective) individual. However, each of the developmental levels, lines, states, and self can be viewed from four perspectives, which Wilber calls *the four quadrants*. In fact, according to Wilber, in order for an approach to be considered truly integral, it must consider all quadrants, all levels, all lines, all states, a model referred as "all-quadrant, all-level" or "AQAL" for short (1999b).

As illustrated in Figure 1.1, the four quadrants in humans can be briefly described as follows (Wilber, 1999; 2002a; 2000b):

- **"I": Interior-individual**—Intentional, subjective. Describes psychological levels from prehension and sensation, thru perception, emotion, and concepts, to formal operations, vision-logic and transpersonal stages. Also includes the waves and tiers of Spiral Dynamics, from instinctual, magic, and egocentric through sensitive, integral, and holistic self.
- **"It": Exterior-individual**—Behavioral, objective. Describes the brain and organism, from organic states to the triune brain to the complex neocortex.
- **"We": Interior-collective**—Cultural, intersubjective. Describes worldviews ranging from archaic and animistic-magical through scientific-rational to pluralistic, integral and holonic. Also encompasses premodern, modern, and postmodern views.
- **"Its": Exterior-collective**—Social, relational. Describes social systems and environments: clans, tribes, empires, nations, states, value communities, integral commons, and holistic meshworks (also described as foraging, horticultural, agrarian, industrial, and informational societies).

Wilber states:
The integral approach is thus constantly on hand to point out all of the correlations of the exterior events in brain and body (the Upper-Right quadrant studied by cognitive science and evolutionary psychology) with the interior events in mind and consciousness (the Upper-Left quadrant studied by interior psychologies), and to further show how all of them are inescapably anchored in cultural and social realities as well (the Lower-Left and Lower-Right quadrants)—with none of those quadrants being reducible to the others (2000c, p.24).

Development, therefore, can be described as the successive unfolding of human potential at all levels, along all lines, through all states, and in all quadrants, as illustrated in greater detail in Figure 1.2 (below). Well-being, then, is the balancing and integrating, through the self system, of the unfolding developmental lines as is appropriate at each developmental level or stage. Failure to differentiate, transcend, and integrate at any juncture or developmental fulcrum is what leads to pathology. The causes of these failures or pathologies, from an integral perspective, must take into account all quadrants: intentional, behavioral, cultural, and social.

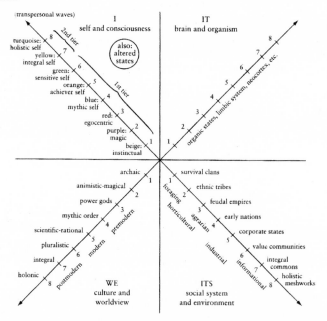

Figure 1.1: Some Examples of the Four Quadrants in Humans
(Wilber, 2000a, p. 43)

Much of Wilber's work, like the preceding descriptions, focuses on the individual. However, in virtually all of his recent books (1996, 1997, 1998, 1999c, 2000a, 2000d), Wilber pays a lot more attention to the collective domain quadrants of culture and social systems. The adaptation into integral theory of Spiral Dynamics, based on the biopsychosocial systems concept of Clare W. Graves (2002), is a very important step toward addressing the worldviews line of development of individuals, groups, organizations and cultures from egocentric to ethnocentric to worldcentric (Beck, 1999; Beck and Cowan, 1996).

The Medicine Wheel as Integral Theory

In the development of my framework for an integral psychology of liberation and transformation, the Lakota medicine wheel model as presented by the Four Worlds Development Project (Bopp, et al., 1989; Bopp, et al., 1998; Bopp and Bopp, 2001) is foundational. Both an intellectual influence and a source of inspiration, the Four Worlds' model helped me tie together many ideas and concepts I had begun to consider since the early 1980s regarding holistic approaches to personal and social transformation. Marilyn Ferguson's "Aquarian Conspiracy" (1980), Jean Houston's human potential and Mystery School work (1982, 2000), and the emergence of transpersonal psychology (Assagioli, 1965/1976, 1973; Walsh, 1984; Walsh and Vaughn, 1980; Wilber, 1977, 1980, 1981) exposed me to holism not only as approach or methodology, but as a paradigm shift for increasing numbers of scholars and practitioners within psychology, philosophy, spirituality, and science. Later, my Master's thesis research revealed to me the emergence of this holistic paradigm in the corporate world as well (Quiñones Rosado, 1989).

Yet, in examining the Four Worlds' medicine wheel model, I realized that this holistic worldview of an emerging New Age movement in the US was still not entirely "whole", as it maintained a primarily individualistic, white, and middle/professional-class orientation, in spite of the strong influences of indigenous American and Asian (though not African) cultures. These New Age or transpersonal approaches, while emphasizing the interdependence of mind, body spirit, and ecosystem, seemed not to give much importance to the oppressive nature of our social, political, economic, and cultural environments. And while concerned with the individual's ability or potential to affect change through personal "empowerment", these approaches for the most part did not take into account the interdependent nature of relationships between society's institutions and its multiple and differentially ranked communities; they seem to ignore the realities of institutional power altogether. The Four Worlds' medicine wheel model forced me to redefine "holism" and the nature of a "holistic worldview."

Wheel symbols representing complex visions of the cosmos and holistic views of growth and healing have been used for thousands of years by indigenous peoples of North and South America, the Caribbean, Africa, South and East Asia, the South Pacific, and ancient Europe (Bopp, et al., 1989; Bopp and Bopp, 2001; Lörler, 1991). Together with the concept of *medicine*, or "any substance, process, teaching, song, story or symbol that helps to restore balance in human beings and their communities" (Bopp et al., 1998, p.18), the *medicine wheel* provides the foundation of a worldview that is significantly broader, deeper and more relevant to our present reality than contemporary models of health, well-being and development, whether mainstream or alternative (Bopp and Bopp, 2001).

An "integrative scheme of thought to guide action" (Bopp et al., 1998, p. 18) the Four Worlds' medicine wheel model presents a set of four interrelated circles, hoops or wholes, each one divided into four parts. These circles represent: the **person**; the **family or clan**; the **community**; and the **wider world**.

Each **person**, according to this model, "has the potential to develop capacities in four interrelated areas of their life" (Bopp and Bopp, 2001, p.23):

- **Mental** — related to the mind, the aspect of the self associated with our cognitive processes, our ability to conceive, reason, think, imagine, wonder; both the logical and creative capacities of the mind allow us to shape and name reality.
- **Emotional** — related to the heart, the aspect of the self associated with affect, our feelings and desires; our emotions are what allow us to effectively interact with other individuals, and are key to learning, problem-solving, and survival itself.
- **Physical** — the aspect of the self associated with the body and all its physiological functions, which allow us to interact directly in the world.
- **Spiritual** — related to the spirit, the aspect of the self associated with one's virtues and values, morals, principles, convictions, and life purpose; also associated with intuition and our sense of an intimate relatedness and/or connection to other beings, the planet, and a universal transcendental consciousness (Bopp and Bopp, 2001; Quiñones-Rosado and Barreto Cortéz, 2002).

These four aspects are intimately related and are inseparable; they coexist holistically, or even holographically, each aspect intrinsically linked to and contained within all others. For example, a person's mind and emotions do not exist (or arise) independently of the biochemical and electromagnetic processes in the physical brain, which in turn, depends on other many and complex functions of the body's various systems. Similarly, our perceptions and behaviors (physical) shape, and are shaped by, our thinking patterns (mental), attitudes (emotional), and values (spirit).

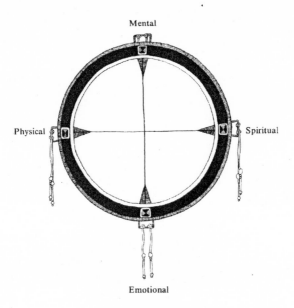

Figure 1.2: The Medicine Wheel: The Person (Source: Bopp et al., 1984/1989, p. 12)

Well-being, according to this model, requires that the four aspects of the personal wheel are equally developed in the well-balanced individual (Bopp et al., 1989). This notion of **balance** among all aspects, central to the tribal concept of medicine, is consistent throughout the four wheels.

The four aspects of constant "activity and potentiality" (Bopp and Bopp, 2001, p. 25) within the **family or clan** wheel are:

- **Dominant thinking patterns** — relates to the primary habits of thinking that inform and drive decisions, arrange collective priorities, and influence power dynamics within the family.

- **Human relations** — relates to the nature and quality of relationships within the family, and the degree to which these support well-being and development.
- **Physical environment and the economy** — relates to the family's ability to meet the physical needs (food, clothes, shelter, safety) of its members.
- **Cultural and spiritual life** — relates to the values, morals and goals of the family, those both held and acted upon; also involves the family's relationship to the Divine and the spiritual and cultural dimensions of life.

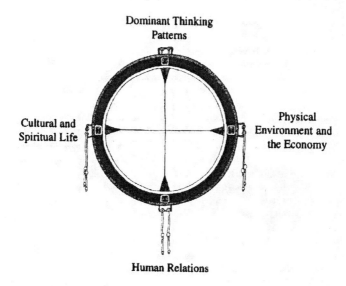

Figure 1.3: The Medicine Wheel: The Family or Clan (Bopp and Bopp, 2001, p. 25)

As individuals are born into, develop within, and are part of families, both the person and the family wheels are encompassed within the **community** wheel, all of which, ideally, are in constant movement toward greater well-being and development. The Four Worlds model maps out the four areas of activity of the community development process as follows:

- **Political and Administrative** — concerned with governance and management of community affairs, and ultimately, how power is arranged.
- **Social** — concerned with patterns of human relations, communications, and conflict resolution.
- **Economic and Environmental** — concerned with the collective economic needs of the community, both immediate and long-term, and in relationship to the natural environment upon which the community depends.
- **Cultural and Spiritual** — concerned with "the prevailing patterns of beliefs, values, morals and goals that constitute the software hidden beneath the surface of the community life" (Bopp and Bopp, 2001, p. 29).

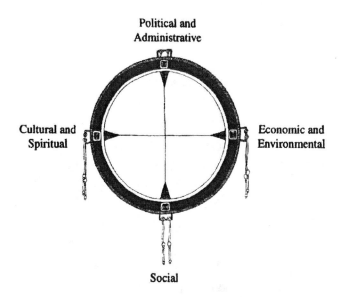

Figure 1.4: The Medicine Wheel: The Community (Source: Bopp et al., 1989, p. 12)

The fourth wheel in the Four Worlds' model encompasses **the wider world**, referring to the larger human society beyond that which is considered the community: the tribe or nation, the state, the country, other countries, and/or regulatory bodies. This is the larger system within which the three previously mentioned wheels exist and to which it is inextricably linked. In considering human well-being and community development at any level, one must also consider these four aspects of the wheel of the world:

- **The Political and Ideological Environment** — refers to the bureaucratic realities and policies at local, regional, national, international levels, as well as the social, political and economic ideological forces.

- **The Social Environment** — refers to behavior patterns and social dynamics affecting the community, such as racism, sexism, and classism.
- **The Economic and Ecological Environment** — refers to the larger economic and environmental conditions that affect the community's development.
- **The Cultural Environment** — refers to "the tension between the dominant culture and the culture of the developing community" (Bopp et al., 1989, p. 32), as well as the organizational cultures of business and governmental institutions that impact the community, the family and the person.

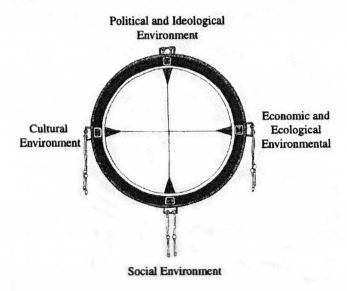

Figure 1.5: The Medicine Wheel: The Wider World (Source: Bopp and Bopp, 2001, p. 25)

The four wheels together provide a basic framework for human and community development. This larger wheel "turns" through certain key processes and dynamics of change: vision, imagination, learning, and volition/participation (Bopp and Bopp, 2001, p.36).

Here, **vision** refers to our capacity to project into the future, to visualize the possibilities of a better life, albeit after critical examination of the present realities in the context of the four wheels. **Volition** refers to will power. At the personal level, volition involves the exercise of attention, choice, and persistent action towards one's specific goals or larger vision. Will at the community level is referred to as **participation**, the meaningful involvement of those impacted by conditions and actively engaged in the processes toward the collective vision.

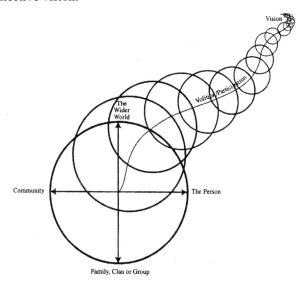

Figure 1.6: The Medicine Wheel: Volition and Vision (Source: Bopp and Bopp, 2001, p. 35)

The basic framework of the Four Worlds' medicine wheel model outlined here, together with a set of guiding principles and culturally-derived tools and strategies, provide a strong foundation for the community work of the Four Worlds International Institute for Human and Community Development in Canada and with indigenous communities throughout the world. As will be evident in the following chapters, the approach I present builds upon this sturdy framework. Though some adaptations are made, I retain the core concepts and symbols that so effectively represent them.

Closing Comments

The similarities between the Four Worlds' medicine wheel model and Wilber's integral theory, particularly the AQAL model, are remarkable: a four quadrants perspective; inclusion of the individual and the collective; acknowledgement of the physical, mental, emotional, spiritual (though Wilber prefers the 3-level body-mind-spirit or a 13-level alternative); and most importantly, understanding of the integral or integrative nature of life and reality inclusive of, yet beyond, human experience.

As could be expected, over the past 25-plus years of his career, Wilber has attracted numerous critics, both advocates and detractors. Recent critiques challenge aspects of his work, including his view of integral transformative practice (Ferrer, 2003), the validity of his integral "theory of everything" (Meyerhoff, 2005, 2006), and even his attitude toward his critics and the impact this attitude has on the continued development of integral theory itself (Visser, 2006a, 2006b). Most relevant to aspects of my research not addressed in this book are Cowan's (2005) strong objections to Wilber's alleged over-simplification of Spiral Dynamics (Beck and Cowan, 1996; Cowan and Todorovic, 2000), an approach co-developed by Cowan based on the work of Clare Graves (2002).

My own critique of Wilber's work that is directly relevant to this text relates to its failure to include social group identity development as one of the multiple developmental lines identified as crucial for the overall development of consciousness, both at individual and collective levels. According to Wilber (1999b), the "important developmental streams" (p. 574), are: the self; morals; motivation; worldviews; affect; aesthetics; cognition; and gender identity (pp. 574-560). However, by gender identity, he refers to development only in terms of the stage progression he developed for this line: morphological (genetic givens); undifferentiated; differentiated (basic gender identity); gender conventionality; gender consistency (norms); gender androgyny (transdifferentiated); archetypal gender union (tantra); and beyond gender (p. 642). Neither here nor elsewhere does Wilber even mention social identity development as an important developmental line, much less address its relationship to, and/or as a function of, oppression.

And while a core theme of integral theory is sociocultural evolution and the overall evolution of consciousness from fragmented (egocentric and ethnocentric) perspectives to integral (worldcentric and cosmos-centric) worldviews, Wilber's failure to acknowledge and understand the importance of social identity development is, precisely, what gives rise to his inability to effectively respond to differential power and oppression, and to adequately address these issues.

Despite these serious omissions, Wilber's integral psychology and larger integral theory provide a vast, invaluable, and most useful synthesis of knowledge that has contributed substantively to the development of my own framework. Wilber, more than anyone I have researched, has created an approach that effectively ties together knowledge regarding the mental, physical, spiritual and emotional aspects of the individual; although he has yet to achieve the same level of depth and cohesion in his analysis of the political, economic, social and cultural aspects of the collective dimension, his AQAL (all quadrants, all levels) model, at least, provides a framework upon which he and/or others can build.

The Four Worlds' medicine wheel approach to community development does address race dynamics and cultural dominance (Bopp and Bopp, 2001), as it also addresses the need of Aboriginal communities to heal from collective trauma caused by oppression (Bopp et al., 1998). Like Wilber's model, however, it does not feature social identity development as such. Despite the absence of this key aspect of development, the basic concepts and visual representations central to the Four Worlds' medicine wheel model helped me fundamentally and permanently transform a previously held fragmented view of human development in the context of social (collective) realities.

Building upon both the Four Worlds' and Wilber's integral models, in the following pages I offer an alternative framework toward an integral psychology of liberation and transformation. The framework introduced in Chapter 2 represents a synthesis of the key aspects of both models, combined with other influences from psychology and social theory.

While drawing from these various sources of knowledge, this framework does not seek to integrate all of the many important aspects of either the Four Worlds' model nor Wilber's integral theory; some elements are adapted or altogether altered, while others remain intact; some are omitted as not immediately relevant. This framework by design, therefore, neither attempts nor intends to address *all lines* of development (e.g., biological, ego, cognitive, needs, moral judgment, worldviews, spiritual) nor *all states* (e.g., states of higher consciousness) sought to be addressed in AQAL model. Given the scope (or self-imposed parameters) of this work, not even all of the social identity development "lines" (e.g., race, gender, sexuality, class, nationality, and others) are fully and equally addressed. Instead, as an effort ultimately aimed at helping people organize toward social transformation, the framework I propose deals with areas not addressed by either model, significantly among them, social identity development. Nonetheless, I do hope to remain faithful to an integral orientation, an attitude that upholds the interrelated and dynamic nature of the whole of life.

Chapter 2
Reworking the Frame

In Chapter 1, I presented some of the key features of integral theory (and integral psychology) and the Four World's medicine wheel model as they pertain to, and influence, the scope of my own theoretical framework for an integral psychology of liberation and transformation. As a framework, this conceptual model seeks to construct (or recreate) a frame, the foundation and pillars upon which a solid structure is built and, hopefully, subsequently modified. This work, as I have indicated, builds upon the work—and stands upon the shoulders—of many others.

In this chapter, I begin to share my framework by presenting an adaptation of the Four Worlds' medicine wheel model, complemented with elements from other models, theories, and approaches in psychology, sociology, social theory, and Wilber's integral theory. This introduction to the framework maps out the basic structures and processes of well-being and development; the dynamics that negatively impact these structures and hinder these processes are addressed in subsequent chapters.

Like other frameworks, this map seeks to allow transformation workers to "frame the work," and in some instances, to "reframe" it, in the psychotherapeutic sense of the word: to redefine perceptions, to re-orient perspectives, to redraw boundaries, for the purpose of shifting one's meanings and behaviors (Bandler, 1985, 1993; Bodenhamer and Hall, 2000; Dilts, 1990).

At the same time, this conceptual model seeks to allow change agents to "work the frame." As an amateur photographer, I often think of this model as a viewfinder, that tiny glass window on the back of a camera. That viewfinder, with its finely etched crosshairs in the center and rectangular frame at the outer borders, is what allows me to center, focus, and compose my pictures; it helps me choose among the many possible shots. Like a viewfinder, this framework allows me to be aware of the larger picture of human activity, while aiding me as I consciously, intentionally, choose where it is that I need to zoom in and focus, or when I need to zoom out to pan or scan the larger field of awareness and activity. In this way, the framework encourages me to create larger or smaller frames, or frames within frames, or multiple interconnected or overlapping frames throughout the sphere of human activity as I seek to explore, examine, understand, and respond to the dynamics therein. In fact, that is what I have done.

Therefore, the graphic used to represent the Sphere of Human Activity (Figure 2.1), is similar to a viewfinder as it has very specific etchings on its broad, circular, and transparent surface. In the center are the crosshairs that help us frame and focus our attention on the individual and/or collective dimensions of human activity within the sphere of being. Simultaneously, these lines help us distinguish or differentiate (more than separate or divide) these dimensions into their particular aspects or facets.

Like the medicine wheel model and, to a lesser extent, integral theory, this model relies on circles or spheres to represent holons (wholes within wholes), contexts, categories, or developmental stages. Meanwhile, spirals are used to represent cycles, movement, or processes.

The Sphere of Human Activity

The Sphere of Human Activity, adapted from the medicine wheel model, is the central element of this integral framework. Indeed, Figure 2.1 (below) looks very much like the medicine wheel depicted in Chapter 1, as it integrates the *individual dimension* (Figure 1.2: MW-The Person) and the *collective dimension* (Figures 1.3: MW-The Family or Clan; 1.4: MW-The Community; and 1.5: MW-The Wider World).

As with the Four Worlds' model, both the personal and collective dimensions of the Sphere of Human Activity coexist in a dynamic, interdependent relationship: individuals live and develop within the collective, while the collective is created and nurtured by the persons who comprise it.

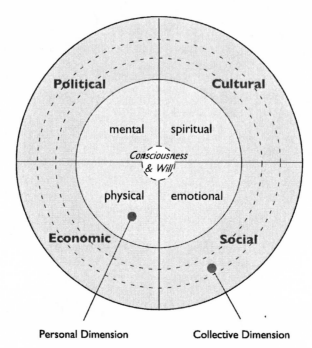

Figure 2.1: The Sphere of Human Activity (adapted from Bopp et al. 1984/1986)

Not illustrated here, as they are outside the scope of this text, the Sphere of Human Activity is one many spheres of being contained within at least two other equally important spheres: the **bio-physical sphere,** which encompasses the planet and the entire universe; and the **meta-physical sphere**, or "The Great Nest of Being[1]" which encompasses "wholes within wholes within wholes indefinitely, reaching from dirt to Divinity" (Wilber, 2000d, p. 437).

---

[1] A Buddhist metaphor used to describe the "container" in which every-thing exists, the context in which everything—objective and subjective—arises.

Consciousness and Will

A distinctive feature of this framework is the inclusion of a center circle, or core, to indicate two primary functions of the self-system: consciousness and will. In this context, *consciousness* refers to our capacity to be aware, while *will* refers to our ability to mobilize our mental, physical, emotional, and spiritual functions. Put another way, consciousness is awareness, and will is that which points our awareness. Furthermore, will is what enables us to "pay attention," to focus, in effect choosing among the countless "objects" within the field of awareness (Assagioli, 1965/1976; Firman and Gila, 2002).

If consciousness is the source of attention, will is the source of intention and the guide of its direction. Consciousness and will, together, allow us to consider options, make decisions, and take action, thus, giving us the ability to use and mediate between different, and sometime competing, aspects of both the individual and collective dimensions of life. Consciousness and will are what allow us to utilize our mental, physical, emotional, and spiritual resources for our personal well-being and collective development (Assagioli, 1976; Firman and Gila, 2002).

The Personal Dimension

As Figure 2.1 illustrates, there are four key aspects of being at the personal dimension of the Sphere of Human Activity: the **mental** aspect (associated with the mind), the **physical** aspect (associated with the body), the **emotional** aspect (associated with the heart), and the **spiritual** aspect (associated with the spirit). The particular characteristics of these aspects have already been presented in the medicine wheel model in the previous chapter. It is worth emphasizing, however, that this framework, like the Four Worlds' and Wilber's models, assumes a holistic view of interdependent coexistence: that each of these four aspects exists and functions in interdependent relationship to every other aspect.

Furthermore, like the other two reference models, this framework assumes a holistic view of interdependent coexistence between the individual dimension and the collective dimension. As human activity is not limited to the individual dimension, well-being and development are not limited to individual persons. Obviously, individuals live in communities, and belong to groups that organize, and develop structures, policies, and processes and shared purposes that, over time, become institutionalized.

The Collective Dimension

The Sphere of Human Activity represents the four aspects of the *collective dimension*: the **economic**, **political**, **cultural**, and **social**. The **political** refers to the aspect of collective life associated with the laws, structures, and processes by which societies are governed. It encompasses the state and all groups, organizations and institutions in charge of developing, adopting, implementing and/or otherwise seeking to influence these laws, structures and processes (Quiñones Rosado and Barreto-Cortéz, 2002). In terms of power relationships, this is the realm of authority[2] (Quijano, 2000). The political aspect is also associated with ideology, or mental constructs applied to the collective, hence its location relative to the *mental* aspect.

The **cultural** refers to the aspect of collective life associated with the ideas, values, beliefs, attitudes, and behaviors shared by members of particular social groups and/or communities, and by the members of society at large (Quiñones Rosado and Barreto-Cortéz, 2002). This is the domain of collective power and control of subjectivity

---

[2] Peruvian sociologist Aníbal Quijano refers to the four major domains of power (*ámbitos de poder*) in society: authority, subjectivity, work, and sex.

(Quijano, 2000). The cultural aspect is located in the same quadrant as the *spiritual* aspect.

The **social** refers to the aspect of collective life associated with the norms and ways in which people relate as members of families, neighborhoods, communities, organizations, and interact between distinct identity groups (by race, gender, class, ethnicity, etc.) (Quiñones Rosado and Barreto Cortéz, 2002). This is the power sphere of affective relationship[3] (Quijano, 2000). As patterns of social behavior largely reflect collective manifestations of affect, this aspect is located relative to the *emotional* aspect (Barbalet, 2001).

The **economic** refers to the aspect of collective life associated with the production, management, and distribution of the resources[4] of a society. It represents the system that regulates commerce, industry, banking, and other forces within our economic system, including the workforce and consumers (Quiñones Rosado and Barreto Cortéz, 2002). This is the power domain of work (Quijano, 2000). This economic realm is associated with the *physical* aspect, hence its placement relative to the individual dimension circle.

The collective dimension is presented as comprised of three concentric circles. The innermost circle of this dimension is that of **groups**, which includes family, friends, and informal clusters of people that are interpersonally and affectively bonded. This circle's proximity to the individual dimension in the graphic represents a relatively close physical, mental, emotional, and/or spiritual distance between the person and other group members, meaning that the person physically lives close, is similar in ideas, values and worldview, and/or is affectively bonded to others within the family

---

[3] Quijano maintains that the fourth realm of power is "sex"; I tend to view this as a realm of *affective relationship*, which may include sex.

[4] Includes material as well as intellectual resources, particularly as knowledge and creative works are being produced and sold for commercial purposes.

or group. This proximity also represents a relatively high level of interpersonal interdependence in every aspect in both dimensions. For example, family members tend to depend on each other for both money and affection, while also often counting on each other for new information, emotional support, and spiritual guidance, or even perhaps for access to a friend, a job, or a political asset.

Because of the degree of proximity and/or intimacy, this is also the sphere where the greatest potential for mutual influence exists, where people are most likely to be able to influence their relatives and friends, while being most open to their influence (Vygotsky, 1978). This is the context in which personal and group identities are most directly shaped (Abrams and Hogg, 2004; Worchel and Coutant, 2004).

The second circle is that of **communities and organizations**. Montero (2004) defines community as "a group in constant transformation and evolution (its size can vary), that in its interrelation generates a sense of belonging and social identity, with its members gaining awareness of itself as a group, and strengthening itself as a unit and a social potentiality (Montero, 2004, p. 207)," while Prilleltensky (2005) emphasizes a group's sense of community and social power.

Through my organizing work, I have come to view community as a group of people subjectively bonded by a shared identity stemming from a common experience as they move toward a mutual goal. While many people with whom I work see themselves as part of a particular neighborhood, they also may claim membership and identification with groups beyond their locality. For these, community is their workplace, their school, organization or institution: the place(s) where they most often interact with others, use their skills and abilities, express their creativity, talk about family, religion and politics, develop emotional bonds, and derive a sense of purpose. Their sense of connection to and identification with a particular community tends to be framed by what has meaning in relation to their social identity. For instance, I have observed that people engaged in social transformation work, tend to identify with a *community-of-struggle* or multiple *communities-of-struggle*. "A community-of-struggle is created through identification in opposition" (Saldaña Portillo, 2002, p. 304), which, as a concept, is useful in anti-oppression organizing as it points to an awareness of a collective effort to resist, challenge and transform oppression, and moreover, that the struggle and the pain it carries is not merely personal, but a burden shared with others like oneself (Drury, 2003).

While the subjective experience of proximity and intimacy in community may be lesser than at the family or group level, as may be the level of interpersonal interdependence and potential for influence among members, it is in the context of communities and organizations that personal and group identities are further reinforced.

The third, outer-most circle is that of **institutions**. Society's institutions create and maintain an overarching system of rules, norms, policies, and procedures within and across the four aspects or domains of collective life.

Institutions within the political domain are those that establish, maintain, and enforce a system of laws that sanctions and seeks to regulate the conduct of all members of society. Among these are governments with all their agencies and dependencies, and, of course, political parties and their ancillaries (e.g., think tanks, lobbyists, and political action committees), that seek to influence policy within this domain.

Institutions within the economic domain establish and maintain a resource management system that controls the means of production and distribution of resources (Marx, 1888/2002), and seeks control over the people that produce and consume these resources (Quijano, 2000). Among the economic institutions in contemporary society are "big business" enterprises in all areas, including agriculture, manufacture, commerce, finance, energy, insurance, technology, communications, information, education, entertainment, legal and health services.

Institutions within the cultural domain are responsible for sanctioning ideas, beliefs, values, attitudes, feelings, and behaviors considered normative, and for transmitting these from one generation to the next. Among the main institutions responsible for teaching, (re)enforcing, and/or (re)defining the values, beliefs, behaviors, etc., are the educational system (early childhood education centers, schools, colleges, universities, and technical institutes through graduate school), religious institutions (churches, synagogues, temples, and other houses of worship), and mass communications media (from billboards, newspapers and books to movies, television and the Internet).

Institutions within the *social* domain are responsible for sanctioning and/or promoting attitudes about relationships among individuals and between the diverse groups within society. Civic and service organizations, youth and family organizations,, and philanthropic foundations are but some of the major social institutions in the US. However, most often, government agencies, private non-profit organizations, and religious organizations assume this function in the process of providing services to poor people and families in need.

Indeed, there are overlapping and interwoven functions between many institutions within the different domains that further illustrate the interdependent and dynamic nature of relationships within the collective dimension. Furthermore, these political, economic, cultural, and social institutions directly and indirectly affect the lives of all members of society— individuals, organizations, communities, and other institutions.

Similarly, individuals, organizations, communities, and institutions *can and do* also directly and indirectly impact other institutions and the entire system. This interactive dynamic is precisely the nature of the integral system within the sphere of human activity. However, as agents of transformation we must ask ourselves:

> *As this interactive dynamic of interdependent relationships between and within all dimensions, all domains, and all aspects of the Sphere of Human Activity unfolds, does it lead all of society's members toward greater levels of well-being; does it foster the on-going development of individuals, families, groups, communities, organizations, institutions, nations, and ultimately, of humanity?*

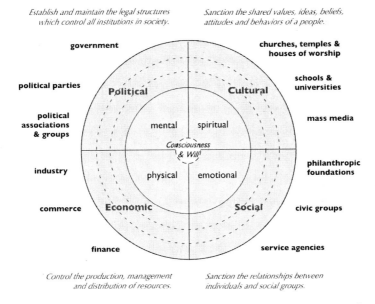

Figure 2.2: Principle Institutions in US and Puerto Rico

Integral Well-Being and Development

Similar to the Medicine wheel model, in this framework *well-being* is approached through **balance**, an on-going process of nurturing and fostering each and all of the aspects of both the personal and the collective dimensions (Bopp et al., 1989; Quiñones Rosado and Barreto-Cortéz, 2002).

At the personal level, greater balance is attained to the extent that a person nurtures her/his mind, body, feelings, and spirit. In order for there to be integral well-being, there must be balanced attention and care throughout one's life. Therefore, there could not be integral well-being in a person whose main activity and life focus is, let's say, her professional career: a person who, in the process, abuses her body with medications, lack of exercise, and improper diet; who neglects her loving relationships; someone who has long forgotten her cultural values of service to family and community. Persons committed to their integral well-being take good care of their bodies, engage their loved ones, and honor their principles, all while attending their intellectual and professional development.

Of equal importance to balance in the process of integral well-being is the principle of **harmony**. Harmony refers to congruence between all aspects of both dimensions. At the personal level, this principle affirms the need for consistency between our ideas and beliefs (mental aspect), our values (the spiritual), our feelings and attitudes (the emotional) and our speech and actions (the physical). It is the principle captured in the popular phrases, "Practicing what you preach," or "Walking the talk." It is embodied in the on-going struggle to resolve those internal contradictions or conflicts between what we think, feel, believe, and do.

At the collective level, harmony is reflected in the congruence or consistency between the laws of a society (political), expression of its values (culture), the quality of relationships in community (social), and dynamics in the workplace and marketplace (economic).

Therefore, in this framework, well-being is a state of relative balance (equilibrium) and harmony (congruence) among all of the aspects across both dimensions within the sphere of life.

Sustained states of balance and harmony among all basic aspects lead toward greater integrity. The greater one's ability to sustain balance and harmony throughout the range of conditions and circumstances of life, the greater the degree of integrity in one's particular stage of development.

Here, the concept of integrity has several connotations. One of these alludes to the mathematical concept of the integer, oneness, unity, the union of potentially fragmented parts. Another meaning of integrity is the one commonly used to refer to a person of high moral standing or incorruptibility. Yet, another refers to the architectural concept of "structural integrity," which refers to the synergistic strength obtained by the strategic and precise placement of the different elements of construction.

This integrity, this unity beyond fragmentation, this incorruptible character, this synergy, gives a person an ability, a capacity, a mental, emotional, physical and spiritual strength to lead their life with ever-increasing levels of well-being and development of their potential. Integrity in this broader sense is the basis of what can be called personal power or authentic power. It is the source of what we refer to as true empowerment that may become authentic or transformative leadership.

Consciousness and will play a key role in the process toward integral well-being, since it is through our capacity of self-awareness and the ability to direct our actions that we can create change in our lives. Our consciousness allows us to become aware of the internal conflicts and contradictions as they arise; our will enables us to take the necessary corrective action. This way, we mobilize and utilize the internal resources of each of the four aspects of our being for the purpose of enhancing our personal well-being. Moreover, through our individual consciousness and will, we can identify, and seek to mobilize and utilize the external resources in the collective realm we may need to further our survival, growth and beyond—our development.

While *well-being* refers to a relative state of integrity in a given moment or stage of life, *development* refers to the movement through the stages of growth throughout life, over time (Beck and Cowan, 1996; Berry, 2002; Wade, 1996; Wilber, 1980). Therefore, development involves a future orientation in time, but is always based upon the stages already attained in the past.

As at the personal dimension, balance, harmony, and the ensuing integrity are also essential to the well-being and development of the collective. In similar fashion, a society (or a particular community or group within a society) must use its collective consciousness and will to address its political, economic, social, and cultural needs and future goals.

By collective consciousness and will I mean, not only the sum of the personal self-awareness of individuals and their particular capacities to direct their own actions; by collective consciousness and will I mean the synergistic, group-level awareness and committed participation attained through people's shared experience, through their common history, identity, and purpose. This synergy enables a society, community, or group to identify, mobilize, and utilize all of their resources to meet the needs of the entire collective. Collective consciousness is what, for example, gives a society a sense of national identity on the basis of a shared history and a present experience; collective will is what would have the people of that nation rally together to defend that shared identity, and to protect—or to seek— their sovereignty.

In keeping true to the principle of integrity, collective well-being and development are attained, maintained and advanced by continually striving for congruence between the shared ideas, values, feelings, and behaviors of the group(s), and between the potentially competing interests of its political, cultural, social and economic institutions. This, I believe, is what enables a society, community, or group to consciously and skillfully direct its future development, allowing it to be truly self-determining.

Therefore, a key, albeit obvious, principle fundamental to this model is: the greater the level of well-being and development of a society, the greater the level of well-being, development and empowerment of the individuals that comprise it. Simultaneously, I propose that the greater the level of well-being of individuals within a society, then: (1) the greater the level of well-being of the collective in the present; (2) the greater the potential for future development of the collective; and (3) the greater the ability of the collective to be self-determining on an on-going basis.

Identity Development within the Sphere of Life

Within the Sphere of Life, a person develops a complex, dynamic, and context-dependent identity constructed on the basis of: (1) her/his particular *personal* traits and interpersonal experiences; and (2) the traits and experiences generally associated with each of the multiple *social groups* of which that person is a member (Brewer and Hewstone, 2004; Brewer and Gardner, 1996; Kiecolt, 2000; Stryker, 2000).

Identity emerges from the natural processes of the self-system which, as discussed in Chapter 1, is characterized by the self's tendency to identify with the structures, patterns and contents within the field of consciousness. From a cognitive, or more specifically a neuro-linguistic/semantic, perspective (Bodenhamer and Hall, 2000; Hall, Bodenhamer, Bolstad, and Hamblett, 2001), identity can be described as a complex pattern involving mental representations of the self that are tightly linked to language and meanings which are in turn deeply associated with specific emotional and conditioned behavioral responses. Resulting from our human capacity of self-reflexivity, identity appears to develop, at least initially, in linear or sequential fashion: from **self-image,** based primarily on internal visual and kinesthetic representations of the body, the physical location of the sense of self; to **self-concept,** based on auditory-linguistic internal representations associated with this self-image; to **self-esteem,** based on values and layers of meaning ascribed to and linked with the self-concept; to **self-love,** based on cumulative emotional reactions to one's sense of self-worth, self-concept and self-image. [See Figure 2.3.]

As indicated, each step or stage in the process is constructed upon the preceding stage(s), while it also loops back to feed, support or augment the earlier stages. Yet, as with most other processes to be described in this integral model, this process is also a spiraling one; self-love subsequently loops around to further sustain self-image, and onward, ultimately developing into a higher order dynamic network of criss-crossing interactions of great complexity.

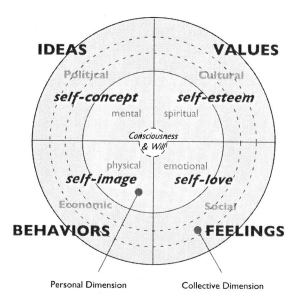

Figure 2.3: Psychosocial Aspects of Integral Well-Being

Both personal identity and social identity emerge as we perceive (through the senses), recognize (name, sort for similarity and difference, etc.), understand (examine, evaluate, and ascribe meaning to) things, events and other people, and respond (emotionally and behaviorally) to others and the world, always in relationship to others.

Personal identity

From this integral perspective, personal identity can be understood as the composite self-image, self-concept, self-evaluation and feelings toward the self which arise from an individual's unique traits and patterns which, in turn, arise from her or his particular physical, cognitive, moral, affective and behavioral aspects as these developed within the economic, political, cultural and social context.

This conception of identity takes into account genetic factors that determine or greatly influence many aspects regarding our physical traits and abilities, our multiple intelligences, and our temperament (Pinker, 2002), as these certainly have an impact on our individual sense of self or personal identity. As a person's sex, skin color, hair texture, and other aspects of their physiology, and verbal-linguistic, logical-mathematical, visual-spatial, auditory-musical, body-kinesthetic, intrapersonal and interpersonal communication skills, and other aptitudes are inherent to the physical and mental aspects of their being, it only makes sense that the self-system identify with these as components of their "I." Yet, as the person is born into and raised within a family, a community, and a larger society that gives particular meanings to, and generates feelings attitudes regarding these traits and capacities, the person internalizes these collectively held meanings, feelings, attitudes and behavior patterns as part of their personal identity.

Additionally, the events we experience, whether as witnesses or participants, inevitably are charged with meanings and feelings we have learned from and internalized within the overall social and cultural context of the collective. Therefore, the "I" of identity, for the most part, is constructed *because of* the dynamic relationship within the economic, political, cultural and social context in which we are raised (Bell, 1997); it is through the process of cultural transmission, which includes socialization, enculturation and acculturation (Berry, Poortinga, Segall, and Dasen, 2002; Gardiner and Kosmitzki, 2002; Stryker, Owens and White, 2000), that identity development occurs.

As Figure 2.3 also illustrates, these social learning processes, engaged both deliberately and unintentionally by members of the family, group, community and institutions, ensure that individuals internalize the *ideas* (and beliefs), *values* (and meanings), *feelings* (and attitudes), and *behav-*

iors (and reactions) of the culture(s) in which they are immersed and carry them on to future generations.

These ideas, values, feelings and behaviors are culturally bound to language: that through which we name and give meaning to particular images of self, or to assign value or worth, albeit always relative to other people and things; that through which, within the collective context, particular emotional charges are stimulated, neuro-linguistically associated, and triggered again, in relation to the aspects of our perceived "self" or "I." Therefore, the personal dimension of identity can only arise within the overall social and cultural context of the collective, if not for anything else, because language, so central to how we internally represent our self to ourselves and to others around us, is both a product and an instrument of culture (Jacobs, Bleeker, and Constantino, 2003; Vygotsky, 1978).

Social Group Identity

No less important within the dynamic interaction between the individual and the collective in the process of identity formation is how the person is perceived, named, valued and responded to by others within their social environment. Given our tendency to sort information for sameness and difference, together with our propensity to generalize, delete and distort that which we perceive (Bodenhamer and Hall, 2000), it is not surprising that societies create classifications of people into social groups. Thus, it is not surprising that in their first years children already have a basic awareness of gender and race, and their membership in these social groupings (Tatum, 1997). This membership or sense of belonging, of being a part of a group, and the group—along with its characteristics—being of part of oneself, is another central aspect of identity (Stryker et al., 2000).

As an anti-oppression approach for integral well-being and development, this framework is most concerned with social group identity and its centrality in the overall process of liberation and transformation. In this context, and throughout this book, social identity categories refer to those that differentiate people in ways that are significant for the impact these designations have on their lives. These categories are based on "differences that make a difference," as my anti-oppression organizational development colleagues at Elsie Y. Cross Associates like to say.

Among the social group identity categories of major impact in contemporary US society are *gender, class, race, nationality, ethnicity, sexuality, and religion.* While *political affiliation* along the conservative-liberal-radical continuum has also been a relevant social identity at given times in US history, e.g., the McCarthy period, it is not generally considered a social group identity. However, within the context of Puerto Rico's colonial relationship with the US, political affiliation as defined by a person's stated ideology regarding the islands' political status[5], is most definitely a major identity category. Two other important identity categories not represented in Figure 2.4 are *age* and *ability* (both mental and physical); the main reason for not including these in the graphic is merely aesthetic, to keep the graphic a bit less visually complex.

---

[5] Political ideology in the Puerto Rican archipelago relates primarily to the three historically proposed options to its colonial status: statehood, some version of the current "Commonwealth" (territory or possession), and independence.

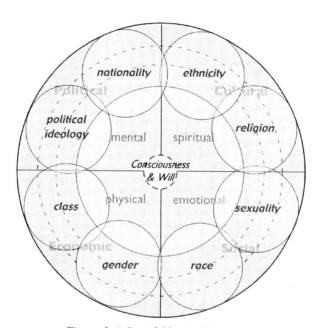

Figure 2.4: Social Identity Categories

In Figure 2.4, social identity categories are placed within the collective dimension though crossing into the individual dimension, so as to illustrate that all social identities form part of the individual's personal identity. The circles depicting distinct social identities also overlap with one another, so as to indicate that these identities intersect and, moreover, coexist in the dynamic interrelationship.[6]

Within these major social identity categories are the specific social identity groups. These social identities have direct bearing on an individual's or group's ability to attain

---

[6] A more accurate, albeit visually cluttered, representation might include criss-crossing lines to illustrate an elaborate web of connections between all social identities, such as in Figure 3.1: The Matrix of Domination, p. 84.

and maintain an adequate level of well-being and development. These categories are subdivided into specific social identity groups:

- **Gender** — men, women, transgendered people
- **Class** — owning class, professional/middle class, lower middle/working class, low-income/poverty class (Leondar-Wright, 2005)
- **Race** — white, Asian, indigenous, Black, Latino/Hispanic (Quiñones-Rosado, 2002)
- **Nationality** — US American, Canadian, British, Mexican, Puerto Rican, Dominican, etc.
- **Ethnicity** — European-American (of English, Irish, Italian, German, Jewish, etc., *cultural* lineage), Asian-American (Japanese, Chinese, Korean, Vietnamese, Indian, Pakistani, etc.), Native American (Lakota, Chippewa, Navajo, Cherokee, and hundreds of other cultural groups), African-American,[7] Latino (Mexican, Chicano, Puerto Rican, Cuban, Salvadoran, etc.)[8]
- **Sexuality** — heterosexual, gay, lesbian, bisexual, transsexual
- **Religion** — Christian, Jewish, Hindu, Buddhist, Muslim, Wiccan, Yoruba, etc.
- **Political Affiliation** — pro-status quo (Republican, Democrat), radicals (greens, communists, socialists, separatists or pro-independence nationalists)

---

[7] Though many African-Americans are descendantsof west African peoples, the many different cultural (religious and linguistic) groups throughout the region were deliberately mixed by slave traffickers and owners during slavery in order to break psychological ties with the Motherland and to undermine social, and potentially political, ties among slaves. This has resulted in that many Africans in the diaspora today are often unable to precisely identify their specific cultural lineage.

[8] As with race, ethnicity, as a social identity category in which Latinos/as find (and must define) ourselves, raises issues that point to the complexity and controversy of the term. For the moment, let us say that "Latino" is used an umbrella term for cultural identity groups with origins in Latin America (Quiñones-Rosado, 1998).

- **Age** — adults (ages 21-60), elders (ages 60+), children (ages 0-20)
- **Physical/Mental/Developmental Ability** — abled, persons with disabilities

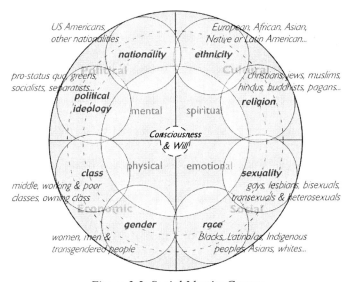

Figure 2.5: Social Identity Groups

While all of these (and surely other) social group identities, together with the traits associated with personal identity, comprise the overall sense of who we are, these multiple identities are not always present in the foreground of our awareness. As it is extremely difficult, if not impossible, to maintain our awareness of all these multiple identities in any given moment, we are only aware of one, two or few of them at a time. In the next chapter I will address issues such as social identity saliency and its contextual nature, and moreover the process of social identity development. Yet all of these issues are addressed within the context of oppression: institutional, interpersonal, and internalized.

Closing Comments

In this chapter, I have presented key aspects of my framework, adopting key concepts and adapting fundamental elements of the Four Worlds' medicine wheel model and within a holistic and developmental approach as proposed by Wilber's integral theory.

The main purpose has been to frame the basic concepts, structures and processes within the dynamic sphere of human activity to be used throughout this work. Key among these is the concept of well-being as on-going movement toward balance (equilibrium) and harmony (congruence) involving all aspects in both individual and collective dimensions of life. Consistent states of relative well-being (integrity) allow development to more inclusive stages of growth along a continuum. It is through consciousness and will that we can use our strengths and mobilize our resources (both internal and external) to address the challenges and overcome the obstacles (either internal or external) we will inevitably encounter in our lives. This basic process is essentially the same for both individual well-being and development as it is for groups, communities, organizations, institutions, and society at large (Beck, 1999; Beck and Cowan, 1996; Bopp et al., 1998; Bopp and Bopp, 2001; Graves, 2002; Wilber, 2000a).

While this process is ostensibly evolutionary, leading to ever greater levels of integrity, it is not linear in direction (toward future goals/milestones), nor necessarily constant in speed (rate of growth). Instead, as Graves (2002) describes, it is a spiraling, oscillating, pulsating process. The well integrated person (or community) tends to be oriented in present time, with a vision of the future that is congruent with their self-in-community, and whose present actions take into ac-

count their personal and collective history. Their basic attitude in life might be expressed as: "Here I stand upon the
shoulders of my ancestors as I move toward ever-greater integrity for the benefit of all beings."

Further, this chapter has sought to firmly establish basic symbols to be used throughout this work, most promi-
nently: the circle to represent wholes, systems, spheres and/or
contexts; and the spiral to represent processes, cycles, and
movement through states of consciousness and/or stages of
development.

Figure 2.6 (below) provides an overview of the process toward well-being and development. However, it hardly
represents the dynamics and the very real challenges of the
world in which we live—the forces that hinder well-being
and development—which shall be presented in the next chapter.

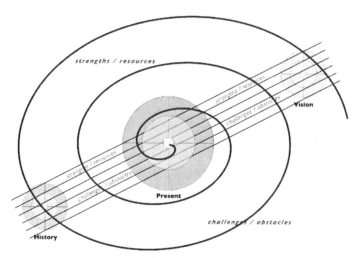

Figure 2.6: Toward Integral Well-Being and Development

Chapter 3
The Forces That Hinder

To transform a situation of oppression requires at once a relentless confrontation of oppressors without, who are often impervious to appeals to reason or compassion, and an equally determined confrontation of the oppressor within, whose violence can unleash a vicious cycle of autodestruction to the self as well as to the group. For without this dual confrontation, the search for personal harmony remains elusive, madness becomes rampant even through sanctioned normalcy, interpersonal violence persists even among loved ones, and death in its various forms remains pervasive.

Hussein A. Bulhan
Frantz Fanon and the Psychology of Oppression
(1985, p. 277)

If the overview of integral well-being and development presented so far can serve as a framework of states and stages to which we might aspire as individuals and a society, it can also serve as an instrument with which to assess and analyze our current reality. In this chapter, I will use my integral model to illustrate the forces that hinder well-being and development, namely oppression in its many forms. In doing so, I will not be elaborating a new theory of oppression nor necessarily adding to the depth of analysis of its various forms done so well by so many others before me. Instead, what I will do is to continue to "work the frame" provided by the integral model to illustrate connections and relationships between the oppressions. In addition, using the Sphere of Human Activity frame as a backdrop, I will discuss various psychosocial processes involved in the dynamics of oppression.

Toward An Integral Analysis of Oppression

When we ask ourselves, or better yet, ask people in our communities of struggle, if there is evidence of integral balance and harmony in their lives the answer is invariably in the negative. In workshops and other organizing activities I conduct, participants generally describe in great detail the visible, external conditions in which they live and work, as well as the internal, subjective realities they personally experience. When asked further, they also describe relationships among people and issues between groups in the various social contexts of their daily lives. Naturally, they describe things both negative and positive, elements that are very difficult and others that are nurturing and sustaining. Some believe that life conditions now, however difficult, may be better for them than they were for their parents and previous generations. Others agree that they may also be even better off than others in communities in other countries, or relative to other groups in their own. Yet still, the consensus is that people, overall, do not enjoy integral well-being in their lives.

In fact, for most people with whom I have worked over the past two decades, life is more about attaining and/or maintaining a relative level of subsistence or survival, not about integral well-being and development. For instance, for a woman living with (or attempting a life without) a violently abusive man, the idea of finding or creating more balance and harmony in her life may be far removed from the immediacy of her struggle to protect herself and her children from physical harm or death. For people in Vieques the goal of stopping the US Navy's bombing of their island far overshadowed any vision of long-term development; now that they have succeeded in expelling the Navy, the community's attention is focused on keeping their homes and land from the grasp of greedy real estate speculators and so-called "developers," and dealing with the high incidence of cancer. And for many Latinos and other People of Color in the US, securing a job, housing, or health services still demands too much effort to sustain a dream of full participation and equal membership in that society.

But why is it that, given the resources and opportunities available to us through the workplace, the marketplace, and countless agencies, organizations, and institutions, many communities of struggle still find it so difficult to successfully get past meeting their most basic survival needs? When asked, people tend to point to other issues: lack of education; low self-esteem; negative attitude; poor language skills; bad work habits; chronic health problems; mental illness. At times, the tone is accusatory, even self-blaming. Nevertheless, people that live, work and struggle in community know that the issues are complex, not only because there are so many, but because people know or sense that these problems are also intertwined and interdependent. Furthermore, they know that these problems are mere symptoms of something more serious.

A similar level of complexity arises in my work with individuals. For example, for an otherwise very effective social worker, her recurring cycles of alcohol dependence, depression and anxiety were experienced as related to such varied issues as childhood sexual molestation, sexual identity, political ideological affiliation, and spiritual emergence, which resulted in isolation from family and friends, absence of affective-sexual relationships, and unemployment. More typical are the women and men so committed (addicted?) to their work in community that they routinely over-extend themselves physically, mentally, emotionally, and even financially at the expense of their health, their families, and relationships beyond the work context—all of whom wrestle with issues, past and present, related to abuse, neglect and multiple forms of oppression.

As oppression at its various levels is central to this discussion, and moreover, to an integral psychology of liberation, it seems appropriate, if not necessary, to define it at this point.

Defining oppression

A working definition of oppression I learned many years ago, and still find useful in introductory workshops, is **prejudice + power = oppression** (Lester and Johnson, 1990, pp. 306-307). In this simple, yet effective, equation *prejudice* refers to more than just unfavorable prior judgments about, say, People of Color, women or poor people based on negative stereotypes, misinformation, distorted history and falsehood; prejudice necessarily involves preconceived notions about whites, men, wealthy people and other privileged groups that are favorable, positive notions that are similarly based on stereotypes, misinformation, distorted history and falsehood. Meanwhile, *power* refers to access to and availability of resources, though trainers with The People's Institute for Survival and Beyond effectively point out that by power they mean "having legitimate access to systems sanctioned by the authority of the state" (Chisom and Washington, 1997, p. 36).

This basic *prejudice + power = oppression* formula can be applied to any of the social identity categories to examine oppression in its many forms. In US and Puerto Rican societies, these forms include: **racism, classism, sexism, heterosexism, eurocentrism, imperialism/colonialism, ageism, ableism,** and domination by virtue of **religion** (including anti-Semitism) and **political-ideological affiliation**.

Defining oppression with more specificity, Hardiman and Jackson (1997) state that "social oppression...is an interlocking system that involves ideological control as well as domination and control of the social institutions and resources of the society, resulting in a condition of privilege for the agent group relative to the disenfranchisement and exploitation of the target group[s]" (p. 17). Hardiman and Jackson go on to specify four key elements necessary for a condition of oppression to exist:

- The agent (oppressor) group has the power and authority to define, name and determine what is "real," "normal," or "correct" within society.
- Differential and unequal treatment of targeted (oppressed) group members is institutionalized and systematic; these forms of behaviors are embedded in social structures and occur consciously and unconsciously.
- The condition of oppression is psychologically internalized by the target group[s] through socialization resulting in their collusion with oppressor's ideology and social system.
- The oppressor's culture is imposed throughout society, while the target group[s'] culture and history [are] misrepresented, discounted, or eradicated (p.17).

Black and Latina feminist thinkers (Hill Collins, 2000; hooks, 2000b; Levins Morales, 1998; Sandoval, 2000), also address the interlocking and dynamic nature of oppression in its many forms. Beyond the intersectionality of oppressions, which speaks to the interrelatedness of sexism, racism, classism and other oppressions in producing injustice, Hill Collins also describes the "matrix of domination...[as] how these intersecting oppressions are actually organized...[within] structural, disciplinary, hegemonic, and interpersonal domains of power" (2000, p. 18).

From an integral perspective, oppression is a system of systems, of sociological forces and psychological dynamics that negatively impact all aspects, all levels, and all dimensions within the Sphere of Human Activity. As Figure 3.1 (see p. 85) illustrates, each system of oppression—

sexism, racism, classism, eurocentrism, and so on—is associated with a specific quadrant within the collective dimension (e.g., nationality within the political; class within the economic; race within the social; or ethnicity within the cultural), as these arguably originate from or pertain primarily to those particular domains.[9] Each of these systems is connected to all other systems, though not hierarchically in relationship to one another and where no single form of oppression (or triad, for that matter) is first or foremost. Together, these systems create an intricate network of structures and self-perpetuating processes that, in effect, constitute an all encompassing matrix of domination.

---

[9] In this model, gender is placed within the economic aspect (which in turn is placed in the same quadrant as the physical aspect) on the basis of biological gender difference and its role historically in the division of labor—a distinction not to be confused with gendered power differential, which like all forms of oppression, is rooted in the complex econo-politico-socio-cultural dynamics within the matrix of domination (Hill Collins, 1990). Race—a social construction made reality that arises from the coincidence of Eurocentrism (cultural), the colonization of the Americas (political), and its emergent slave-based capitalism (economic) (Quijano, 2000)—is placed within this integral-though-primarily-social psychological-framework in the social/emotional quadrant, on the basis of the psychological trauma of racially oppressed peoples, and on social dynamics rooted in instilled fear of Blacks and other People of Color (Leary, 2005; Wineman, 2003). Similarly, sexuality is located in this same quadrant based on social and affective considerations. Placement of the other social identity categories and their corresponding oppressions are more self evident. Having said that, it is important to remember that the map is not the territory, as Korzibski and others have insisted (Hall, 2000), particularly a map that attempts to describe the dynamic, interrelated, holographic nature of relationships between all aspects, dimensions of human activity, including social identity.

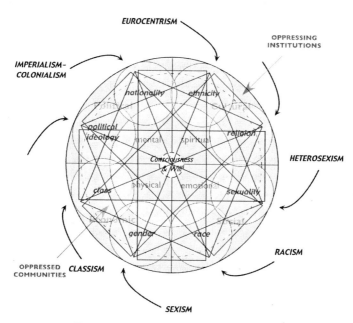

Figure 3.1: The Matrix of Domination

The Cyclone of Oppression

While this "matrix" is represented in Figure 3.1 (above) as a grid of dozens of bi-directional criss-crossed lines of interaction, being from a Caribbean island under the seasonal threat of hurricanes, my natural tendency is to picture and feel the forces of racism, sexism, classism, etc., as the powerful "winds" of a cyclone. Originating from society's many institutions, these circling winds form a powerful vortex that surrounds all aspects of the collective, creating great pressure that spirals inward and encompasses the individual dimension in all its aspects as well.

Beyond the metaphor, this *Cyclone of Oppression* (Figure 3.2, below) provides a useful visual framework

through which to illustrate both the hierarchical power between dominant and subordinated identity groups in each social identity category, and the structural and institutional nature of oppression, while remaining consistent with its non-
hierarchical configuration.

Like all the graphics in the model, Figure 3.2 builds
upon previous graphics (except here I choose not to include
the grid of interconnections of the matrix). Based on Social
Group Categories diagram (Figure 2.5) from the previous
chapter, this figure shows the identity groups within each
category located in oppositional relationships based on institutional power, with the dominant identity groups on the
outer circle and the subordinated groups within the inner part
of this circle. The dominant social groups are placed over and
above the subordinated groups in typical hierarchical fashion
within that circle, both groups visually separated by a dotted
line.[10] Subordinated groups, collectively, appear as a circle
enclosed within the larger outer circle of dominant identity
groups.

---

[10] Actually, as one might say that a circle has no top or bottom, or above
and below, to indicate the hierarchic relationship I chose to locate the
"dominant" or "superior" position in the outer-most part of each circle relative to the center, which appears "above" only at the top of the diagram.

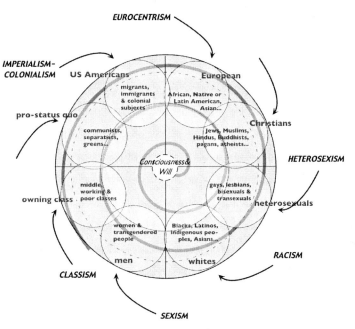

Figure 3.2: The Cyclone of Oppression

With all of the dominant identity groups in the outer-most circle, it is important to notice that this location coincides with the location of the social, economic, political, and cultural institutions as previously illustrated in Figure 2.1 (Sphere of Human Activity) and Figure 2.2 (Primary Institutions in the US & Puerto Rico). This circle of dominant groups, or circle of institutional power, reflects the reality that institutions are created, organized, and directed by people who are *simultaneously members of multiple dominant groups* within their society. In the US, for example, virtually all major economic, political, cultural, and social institutions created during its founding years (and since) were established by and for the benefit of white, owning class, heterosexual,

Christian, pro-American, men of European descent (Zinn, 1995).

Each dominant identity group, backed with state-sanctioned institutional power, generates a form of oppression, or system of hierarchical arrangements of differentially powered individuals, in which multiple-dominant group members are ranked the highest, and as such are generally granted superior positions in society relative to all others.[11] The institutional power to evaluate and rank also points to the legacy of oppression that remains a central factor in the perpetuation of oppression over time.

The Internalization of Oppression within the Culture of Imposition

The shared ideologies, values, feelings, attitudes and behaviors of the dominant identity groups (the cyclone of oppression), together with the structures and dynamics leading to their institutionalization (the matrix of domination)— collectively and historically—are what have given rise to that which can be called the *culture of imposition*. Within this culture of imposition (see Figure 3.3): the ideas and beliefs of the dominant groups coalesce into **imposed ideologies** on members of all groups in a society regardless of other perspectives and ways of thinking; values traditionally held, even by dominant groups' original cultures, become **distorted and corrupted,** yet are upheld as the cultural norms to be abided by by all; **negative feelings,** rooted in fear toward others, become primary motivators, and lead to harmfully competitive, survivalist, and ultimately **destructive be-**

---

[11] A more detailed diagram would also illustrate the relative positions on a continuum along which the subordinated groups are located at any given historical moment, e.g., race: with Asians as currently closest to white, followed by Latinos/as, then Native Americans, and with Blacks historically always at the bottom.

haviors, particularly directed toward subordinated members of oppressed groups within the society (Bulhan, 1985).

In addition to the stereotypes, misinformation, exclusions, rejections, acts of violence, and other harmful ideas, values, feelings and behaviors, a defining feature of this culture is the use of power, whether institutional power or that of personal force, to prevail and maintain one's privileged position. It is this culture of imposition, as opposed to a culture of well-being, that provides the sociological context for the psychological internalization of oppression.

Oppression's Impact on Identity

From a social cognitive perspective, the culture of imposition is internalized through internal representations (as images, sounds, sensations, even smells and tastes) associated with the various social group identities that are instilled and installed[12] in both dominant and subordinated groups members. More importantly, the language and meanings attached to these multi-sensory messages become as much a part of our conscious mind as they do our unconscious.

In the discussion on identity in Chapter 2, it was established how both personal and social identity emerge during and as a result of the process of socialization, developing within the context of dynamic interaction between the person and others in the collective dimension. This process, at one level, involves the formation of identity from self-image to self-concept to self-esteem to self-love, and from there onto higher levels of complexity. Simultaneously, this process involves the internalization of the ideas, values, feelings, and behaviors of the culture(s) in which they are immersed. Each

---

[12] I use the term "install" which is used in NLP and Ericksonian hypnosis in reference to a process by which messages and meanings are deliberately implanted, imbedded, or "suggested" through hypnotic trance. Messages and meanings may also be installed inadvertently by any person, group, or context in others particularly in heightened emotional states.

aspect of the self-system necessarily arises or is created in relationship to others in the social environment.

However, given the pervasiveness of the culture of oppression within the social environment, it is not surprising that socialization results in **negative self-image, limiting self-concept, low self-esteem, and a lack of self-love** for subordinated group members. Conversely, for dominant group members the process results in a positive, albeit, distorted self-image, exaggerated self-concept, inflated self-esteem, and narcissism, particularly when considered relative to subordinated counterparts. From an integral perspective, one must say dominant group members are also negatively impacted.

Since all people simultaneously have (and have had or will have) both dominant and subordinated social identities, all people are impacted. Of course, not all people are impacted equally. Certainly, a person with, say, six out of eight subordinated social identities (e.g., a black, Latina, lesbian, poor, communist, and atheist) experiences oppression differently than someone with, say, two subordinated social identities (e.g., a poor woman, but who is white, US American, Christian, able-bodied, heterosexual, and Republican). Also, not all subordinated social identities are equally weighted in all contexts; some would argue that race, gender and class are "differences that make <u>more</u> of a difference" and weigh more heavily than other oppressions in most social contexts in the US.

The point here, however, is that within the culture of imposition, the self-system is inevitably shaped based on the pre-established images, notions, valuations, attitudes and feelings which presume that the dominant group members and their cultures are the standard by which all people are to be measured.

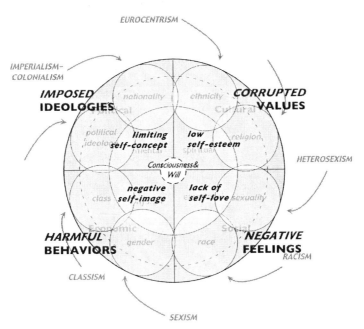

Figure 3.3: Impact of Cultural Oppression on Personal Identity

Oppression's Impact on Affect of Subordinated Identities

Within the culture of imposition, the psychological internali-zation of oppression at the deepest levels of the self-system is inevitable. Albeit at varying degrees and, in some cases, mitigated by supportive families, communities and/or non-traditional institutional supports, everyone is exposed to and socialized in the prevailing generalizations or stereotypes, both favorable and unfavorable, regarding all of the major social group identities. Particularly with today's mass com-munication systems, even in communities where there is little social identity diversity there is plenty of information—all with value-laden messages—about people of other cultures,

nationalities, sexualities, economic classes, religions or political persuasions.

In addition to the impacts on key aspects of personal
identity, internalized inferiority manifests in a sequence of
psychological or intra-psychic patterns. As Figure 3.4 (see p.
94) visually represents, the process of internalization is like a
coil that spirals inward into the psyche. The culture of imposition powerfully impacts the oppressed person as its negative
devises and misuse of power bore their way into all four aspects of the individual dimension (physical, mental, spiritual
and emotional, or P-M-S-E).

These psychological pattern of reactions appear to
develop in a spiraling sequence, roughly, but not necessarily,
in the order illustrated in the graphic, that is: from a **sense of
invisibility** to **confusion** to **doubt** to **pain** to **shame** to **anger**
to **despair** to **powerlessness** to **passiveness** to **helplessness**
to **apathy** to **cynicism** to **hopelessness** to **emotional numbness** to **self-hate** to **self-destructiveness** (Fanon, 1963, 1967;
Freire, 1970; Herman, 1992; Martín-Baró, 1994; Moane,
1999). Along the way, this spiral (as in other processes in the
model) loops back, and generalizes into a dynamic non-linear
system or network.

Incidentally, this spiral of affective reactions could be
superimposed (if not for aesthetic considerations) upon the
previous figure, as, for example: invisibility is linked to negative self-image; confusion and doubt to limited self-concept;
shame, powerlessness and helplessness to low self-esteem;
anger, rage, self-destructiveness and others are linked to lack
of self-love.

This spiraling pattern of psychological reactions to institutional oppression of subordinated group identities encompasses all four aspects (P-M-S-E) and the psychological
functions associated with each. Eventually, the cumulative
impact of oppression (external events and internal reactions)
reaches all the way through to the very core of being: to con-

sciousness and will. This pattern can result in an ever-diminishing self-awareness and a reduced capacity to choose and act. This topic will be explored in the following chapter.

Meanwhile, it is important to also consider some of the manifestations of internalized inferiority in the social environment.

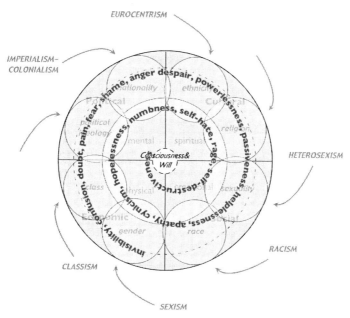

Figure 3.4: Psychological Internalization of Inferiority

Social Manifestations of Internalized Inferiority

The expression of internalized inferiority in the social environment is of particular concern to anyone working toward social change and transformation. Within their social dominance theory, Sidanius and Pratto's (1999) behavioral asymmetry hypothesis suggests that...

Subordinates tend not to act in their own interest to the same extent as dominants do... most often as the result of initial and very dramatic forms of oppression (e.g., slavery, military conquest). Once this oppression extends itself over time, self-debilitating behaviors will arise and then become part of one's normal behavioral repertoire. To a significant degree then, the maintenance of dominance systems also depends on the self-debilitating behaviors of subordinates. More to the point, except for extreme cases of coercion, the persistence of group-based dominance rests on the coordinated and choreographed actions of both dominants and subordinates alike (pp. 306-307).

Hardiman and Jackson's (1997) oppression model and social identity development theory address many manifestations of internalized superiority and inferiority at the various stages of development.[13] Within each identity category, subordinated group members at the acceptance stage of social identity development tend to exhibit the behaviors listed below. This process, represented in Figure 3.5 (see p. 97), is adapted primarily from Hardiman and Jackson (1997, pp. 16-25).

The inner part of the spiral represents the person's subjective or inner process:

- **Adaptation** — in which the person subjectively alters ideas, beliefs, values, attitudes pertinent to her/his social identity group, and behaviorally introduces external changes to important aspects of their native culture, e.g., the use of Santa Claus, reindeer, and snowmen as symbols to celebrate Christmas in Puerto Rico.
- **Rationalization** — in which the person internally explains, justifies and attempts to deal with any cognitive dissonance generated by the changes, e.g., how

---

[13] A table detailing the stages of social identity development appears in Appendix 1.

pretty and progressive[14] it looks to decorate one's home with Santa, reindeer, and snowmen even in our sub-tropical climate, and how children nowadays prefer Santa to the Three Kings anyway, as they have more time to play with their gifts before returning to school.

- **Adoption** — in which the cultural adaptation is adopted or incorporated into the person's ideas, beliefs, values, and behaviors.
- **Identification** — in which the person develops an affinity, an affective connection to, and subjective alignment with the dominant culture; he/she begins to see, think and feel as if a member of the dominant group.

The outer part of the spiral represents the person's attitude, or emotional and behavioral predisposition, within the social context:

- **Accommodation** — in which a person consents to superior position of dominant group members, while attempting to forge a public persona that is acceptable to dominant group members.
- **Collusion** — in which a person actively collaborates with dominant group members in maintaining the system of oppression, even while remaining in a disadvantageous (and dependent) position relative to dominant members; collusion often also involves distrusting, disregarding, discounting, disrespecting, undermining, underestimating, undervaluing, sabotaging, blaming, betraying, etc., of other members of one's own social group (lateral hostility) or members of other oppressed groups (cross-group hostility).

---

[14] Progressive as in modern, but also as in ideologically affiliated with the New Progressive (pro-statehood) Party.

- **Assimilation** — in which the person subjectively and behaviorally integrates the dominant culture, including the ideology of superiority of the dominant group and the presumed inferiority of subordinated groups; the person has adopted and assimilated the values, logic, customs, traditions, modes of worship, etc., of the dominant culture, while rejecting and repudiating ways of life indigenous to her/his own and other subordinated groups.
- **Absorption** — in which a person's subordinated group becomes a part of the dominant group, e.g., Irish, Italians, and Jews acceptance into the white racial construct in the US.

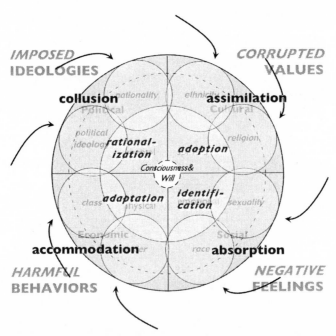

Figure 3.5: Psychosocial Pattern of Internalized Inferiority

Other Observations Regarding Internalized Oppression

In doing anti-oppression work, it is important to be clear about both internalized *superiority* <u>and</u> internalized *inferiority*. For educators and organizers it is important to recognize that, within the system of oppression, it is not just People of Color, women, poor people, gays/lesbians/bisexuals, and other oppressed peoples that have internalized oppression; <u>everyone</u> has been socialized and indoctrinated in the culture of imposition. After all, internalized inferiority can only exist if internalized superiority also exists.

To some extent, internalized superiority and internalized inferiority might be described as the inverse or "mirror images" of each other. We might find that individual dominant group members can also engage in behavioral patterns that are similar to those of subordinated group members: unrealistic expectations of self and others; hostility among members of their own groups; and hostility and violence toward subordinated groups. However, we must remember that, given that the system is designed by dominant group members and for their own benefit, these patterns do not so much limit their ability to maintain their position within institutional hierarchies as they do to advance it, both individually and collectively.

So, even while these are not manifestations and patterns of *all* dominant group members or *all* subordinated group members, there are important distinctions in ways in which internalized oppression is generally expressed by both groups in this oppositional dynamic. Just how subordinated and dominant group members manifest internalized oppression seems to depend on the stages of social identity development at which individuals may be. More specifically, the manifestations and patterns of *internalized inferiority* presented in this chapter tend to be most visible in subordinated group members at the **naïve and passive acceptance stages** of development, and most particularly when in relationship to dominant group individuals, organizations, and institutions.

According to Hardiman and Jackson, as a person gains critical consciousness of the dynamics of oppression and its impact on her, over time she begins to enter the **resistance stage** (first passive, then active). In this resistance stage, the internal psychological manifestations are still present, but are mitigated and mediated to some extent -- by acts of consciousness and will, I would add. While previously she may have merely reacted to an act of oppression against her in fear, shame, despair, and powerlessness, in this stage of resistance she would likely begin to react in anger, passive-aggressiveness, or perhaps even open defiance.

Interestingly, it is not uncommon to see young African Americans and Latinos/as in the US today who, as they enter the **active resistance stage,** deal with their internalized inferiority in ways that seem to parallel manifestations of internalized superiority of some dominant group members in the **active acceptance stage**[15].

Some of these patterns include:
- Creating and publicly displaying "unconventional" cultural expressions in art, music, dance, literature, fashion, etc.
- Attracting attention to themselves through exaggerated visibility, e.g., gangsta look, loud music, highly customized cars, and stylized fingernails.
- Using verbal and non-verbal communications intended to convey arrogance, invulnerability, narcissism, and superiority.
- Demanding visible signs of respect in public settings.

---

[15] In their active resistance stage, dominant group members begin to question, then own, and then reject their own oppressive behavior and attitudes.

These seem not so different than behaviors and attitudes of young (and not so young) white, wealthy men and women who call attention to themselves with luxurious cars, high-tech gadgets, and high profile life-styles, and who seek to set trends with designer clothes, accessories, hair styles, and/or culturally (mis)appropriated art. But as *acts of resistance* of young People of Color, these behaviors and attitudes are still, first and foremost, *reactions* to the culture of imposition and to their personal experiences of oppression. They are attempts to claim power, even if only individually, even if only by adopting ideas, attitudes and behaviors historically used by dominant groups against them, albeit, reframed, transformed, translated to suit their groups' needs and realities.

Psychologically, acts of resistance such as these might be considered defense mechanisms created in attempts to neutralize the pain, shame, fear, and anger of internalized inferiority. Sociologically, they are cultural and economic adaptations designed for survival. Politically, they are expressions against injustice and attempts at change, or at least reform, of institutional racism, classism, sexism, ethnocentrism and other forms of oppression. Spiritually, these may well be expressions that seek "by any means possible" to liberate the soul, perhaps steps intuitively taken in a search to overcome or transcend the limitations placed on us by the material world, albeit, as it has been socially constructed.

These acts of resistance of subordinated members are liberating to the extent that they involve *creative responses* that move beyond mere *unconscious reactions* to oppression, or as in the case of dominant members, the adoption of behaviors, attitudes and trends established by the dominant elite. Beating the system at its own game by adopting the patterns of internalized superiority is certainly not the way the oppressed will be liberated from internalized inferiority, as if these patterns of superiority were antidotes. As we well know—from the vantage point of our own dominant social identities—even while we, in certain contexts, may enjoy relative power and privilege, we are far from being free, ful-filled, or integrally developed. We know, whether intuitively or upon honest introspection, that these patterns of internal-ized superiority are also merely reactive defenses created in order to deal with our own deeply felt-sense of inferiority, separateness, and isolation.

Indeed, like everyone else born into a society that does not necessarily assure their personal existence, dominant group members during childhood have also internalized the images, notions, and felt-sense of being weak, vulnerable, incompetent, helpless—all of which, within their own culture of imposition, are valued as *inferior*. After all, as children we have all learned, to one degree or another, the pain, shame, fear, and anger of being subordinated.

From the perspective of integral well-being, we must also ask: how much balance and harmony can a rich, white, Christian, heterosexual male truly have whose wealth may well have been derived from the forced and unpaid labor of his ancestor's slaves, and whose other privileges stem from the persistent and pervasive institutional inequities still pre-sent today? At some level, even the adult person of privilege socialized in a system that upholds such political, social, and moral notions as "the pursuit of happiness," "all men are cre-ated equal," "liberty and justice for all," "majority rule," "human rights," the Ten Commandments, and other funda-mental values must, at minimum, experience some measure of cognitive dissonance in the realization that: the vast major-ity of people within arguably the world's richest, freest soci-ety do not really, truly have access to the resources that might allow "happiness"; that women, people of color, GLBT peo-ple, the poor, and others are not treated equally or fairly, and do not enjoy the same liberties and rights that might ensure their basic safety and survival; that the majority rules only when convenient to the most privileged few; and that moral law, such as "Thou shall not kill" (or lie, or steal, or covet...) applies only in as much as it protects their privileged position in that society. I would argue that the dissonance, not only cognitive, but spiritual and emotional, is so personal, permanent and pervasive that the basic psychological defense mechanisms—denial, negation, projection, rationalization, compensation, etc.—of the dominant collective are triggered and operationalized throughout society for adoption by all.

Closing comments

In considering the multiple and complex challenges faced by an individual or a community, the integral model becomes a useful instrument of analysis. Whether used to approach the collective or the personal, the model serves as a grid or template to further problematize (Freire, 1970; Shor, 1992) the situation and help us engage in a critical analysis of specific areas of concern while still taking into account the whole.

From an integral perspective, oppression is described as a complex system of systems involving and impacting all aspects and all dimensions within the sphere of human activity. Moreover, oppression is simultaneously a process and structure that supports, aggravates, and/or gives rise to virtually all major problems in society. This "system-of-systems" or matrix of domination can be summarized as:

- **a system of power and privilege** that sanctions and perpetuates dominant-subordinated relationships between social groups and communities through historically established political, economic, social and cultural institutions — a system which, in turn, is supported by...

- **a system of ideologies, values, attitudes, and customs**—*a culture of imposition*—that is collectively shared (albeit, often resisted) by families, communities, organizations, and institutions through cultural transmission processes which continue to define authority, subjectivity, work, and social relations throughout society — which, in turn, is supported by...

- **a system of social group identities** in which people differentially (re)cognize, value, affectively relate to, and behave toward other individuals, groups and communities based on generalizations, distortions and/or omissions attributed to their social identity group(s) (race, gender, class, etc.) — which, in turn, is supported by...
- **a system of core patterns** regarding key psychosocial aspects of identity that is internalized by individuals during their socialization — which, in turn, is supported by...
- **the self-perpetuating, interactive, and non-linear relationships** between all of these systems.

Though this analysis proceeded from the collective level to the individual, ultimately, it is irrelevant where we "begin," insofar as we are clear about the whole picture and how each part relates to the rest. Again, the non-linear (circular, spherical, spiral, or neural) and dynamic (interactive, cross-dimensional, multi-directional, holographic) nature of this matrix—and of this integral model—cannot be emphasized too much nor too often.

Now, upon this analysis of the forces of oppression that hinder well being and development, the following chapter will begin to explore the process of consciousness-in-action.

Chapter 4
Consciousness-in-Action

A psychology of liberation, or a liberation psychology, aims to facilitate social change by providing insights into processes which can aid in the development of a clear analysis, confront the psychological difficulties associated with oppression, and enhance the psychological capacities involved in organizing and taking action.

Geraldine Moane
Gender and Colonialism:
A Psychological Analysis of Oppression and Liberation
(1999, p. 89)

In the previous chapters, I presented the integral model as a framework to be used for assessing well-being within the sphere of human activity, and for critical analysis of conditions and forces of oppression that hinder well-being and development at both the individual and collective dimensions. In this chapter, I use the integral model as a framework to describe the process of change, or more specifically within the culture of oppression and the matrix of domination, the process of consciousness-in-action.

The chapter begins by placing consciousness-in-action in context, both regarding the evolution of the term and concept, and relative to social identity development as an important, yet still unacknowledged developmental line within integral theory.

In this chapter, I go on to describe the process of consciousness-in-action, how it relates to the social identity development model and, more importantly, how it supports the process of development toward liberation and transformation.

Having identified emotional reactivity as a major challenge in the process of consciousness-in-action, I then propose the development of key competencies to positively alter our subjective experience to help move us toward greater responsiveness in the midst of oppression.

Consciousness-in-action in Context

Evolution of the concept

The term emerged out of the work of ilé: Institute for Latino Empowerment[16] as we were looking for a word in English to express Freire's concept of *concientização* (Collins, 1977; Freire, 1970). In Spanish, the terms *concientización* and *concienciación* were familiar to us, terms widely adopted in Latin America for the process of gaining critical awareness or critical consciousness, that which is to replace the false consciousness of internalized inferiority (Freire, 1970; McLaren, 1993). During the early 1990s at the time of ilé's founding, however, we adopted the term *empowerment* (Rappaport, 1981) though reluctantly as it had already begun to be co-opted by both human service providers and organizational development professionals who sought to grant service recipients and workers, respectively, greater participation but without greater power.

Meanwhile, in the anti-racism and anti-oppression contexts in which ilé became involved, we observed that *concientización* tended to be a term more commonly used to de-

---

[16] Mentioned previously, ilé: Institute for Latino Empowerment is a non-profit organization dedicated to anti-oppression community organizing and Latino/a leadership development is the US and Puerto Rico which I founded and co-directed from 1992 to 2005. Initially known by the achronym ILE, our staff and advisory board subsequently adopted the Yoruba word "ilé" (house) as its official name. Currently, the organization has adopted the name ilé: Organizers for Consciousness-in-Action / *ilé: Organizadoras/es para la Conciencia-en-acción*, yet has become known colleagues and community members with whom we work simply as "ilé".

scribe a *subjective* stage of political awareness, an *interior* quality of an individual, or the process of consciousness-raising itself. In these contexts, a person with critical consciousness was one who had undergone a process of conscientization, or more specifically, radical political education, and had acquired critical analytical skills, albeit from a fragmented perspective. However, the person was not necessarily someone actually involved or experienced in self-determining action, in some measure a reflection of the effectiveness of both the co-optation of "empowerment" efforts and community workers by social service providers and human resource professionals (Prilleltensky and Nelson, 1997), as well as the government infiltration and dismantling of Black, Chicano, Indian, and Puerto Rican liberation movements throughout the 1960s, 70s and 80s (Comisión de Derechos Civiles, 1989; Davis, 1998; James, 1998).

Within a short time, however, at ilé we began to use the phrase *conciencia y acción* (consciousness and action) as our translation of *empowerment* to explicitly acknowledge our orientation to leadership development and community organizing, and moreover, to re-establish the importance of <u>action</u> in processes geared toward personal empowerment, community self-determination, collective liberation, and social-cultural transformation. *Conciencia y acción* was also adopted as a deliberate act of resistance to the unnecessary neologisms (e.g., *empoderamiento* or *apoderamiento*) that began to appear in Latino communities in the US, in Puerto Rico and elsewhere in Latin America as the Spanish language translation of *empowerment* (Montero, 2003).

In time, as we became even more involved in Latino community organizing and broader anti-oppression social movements, the need to further differentiate between merely "having" political consciousness or "possessing" critical awareness and actually being engaged in the praxis of *conciencia y acción* became painfully evident. Sadly, we noticed a widespread sense of cynicism and hopelessness among highly conscientized veteran liberation advocates, again, the result of governmental persecution and institutional co-optation of liberation movements, methodologies, and leaders. At the same time, however, in anti-oppression community organizing and organizational transformational efforts where people were actively engaged in change processes, those of us with ilé consistently observed the on-going development of individuals, groups, organizations and communities toward greater self-determination and transformation, the victorious struggle in Vieques being one of the most notable examples. This observation has led me to realize, like Freire and others some time ago, that critical consciousness is not, in and of itself, liberating; consciousness without action only leads to cynicism. It is consciousness-in-action—*conciencia-en-acción*—nurtured by a vision and a sense of hope, that can lead to liberation and transformation.

Consciousness-in-Action, and Social Identity Development Theory

As a process toward liberation, transformation and integral well-being, consciousness-in-action is compatible with Hardiman and Jackson's (1997) social identity development theory. Introduced in the previous chapter (also see Appendix A), social identity development theory presents a generic and functional developmental model applicable to the multiple social group identities (Adams, Bell, and Griffin, 1997). The Hardiman-Jackson model, in effect, presents a liberation process through the developmental stages: from naïve to acceptance to resistance to redefinition to internalization.

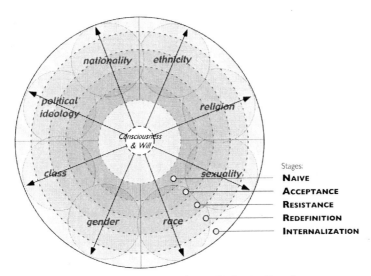

Figure 4.1: Lines & Stages of Social Identity Development

As presented below, consciousness-in-action is engaged as we spiral through each stage of social identity development, a process that is replicated along each identity line.

The Process of Consciousness-in-Action

The forces of oppression, as described in the preceding chapter, can be visualized as the winds of a cyclone spiraling inward from the institutional structures of society, through its organizations and communities, imposing its culture of domination on all social groups, causing tremendous harm to the person's identity and negatively impacting consciousness and will at core of their self-system. Consciousness-in-action, represented in Figure 4.2 (see p. 110), inverts the direction of the spiral. Through acts of consciousness and will sustained over time, consciousness-in-action is a process that is intentionally engaged as people confront oppression for the purpose of moving toward integral well-being. In this process, internalized oppression—both superiority and inferiority—is gradually transformed, healing and regenerating the self-system while collectively co-creating a culture of liberation to uphold the new self.

As indicated in Chapter 2, personal and social identity emerge as we: (1) perceive the self and others through the senses; (2) recognize, name, and sort for sameness and difference; (3) understand and ascribe meaning to self, others and events, and; (4) respond emotionally and behaviorally in society. In Chapter 3, I went on to describe how oppression is internalized throughout socialization as we perceive, name, and assign value and meaning to experiences that disproportionately favor dominant group identities and simultaneously establish their superiority relative to subordinated identities. Further, I indicated that the process of perceiving, naming and valuing was neuro-linguistically linked to emotional and behavioral *reactions* that, from the perspective of subordinated identities, were negative and, ultimately, harmful. These processes were described as being initially sequential, then dynamically interconnected, spiraling outwards in relationship to others and, ultimately, moving forward onto greater levels of complexity.

Following a similar pattern, and building upon the concept of *praxis* (Freire, 1970; Hope and Timmel, 1984), consciousness-in-action involves an on-going process of action-reflection-action. More specifically, the process of consciousness-in-action involves a spiraling process that moves from **perceiving** oppression, **recognizing** and acknowledging its patterns, **understanding** its dynamics and negative impacts, and **responding** effectively to disrupt its course of action. Like other processes described in the model, and like Freire's praxis, consciousness-in-action loops back around and continues the process at higher levels of perception, recognition, analysis, and response. [See Figure 4.2, below.]

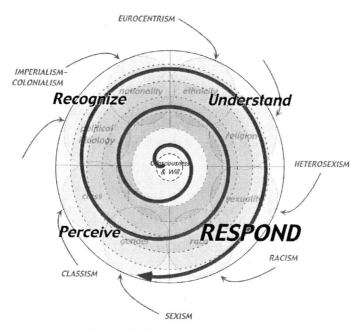

Figure 4.2: Consciousness-in-Action

Perceiving Oppression: Directing Attention, Developing Awareness

As indicated above, consciousness-in-action first requires that people in this process **perceive** oppression in their present reality. They develop a basic perceptual awareness (visual, auditory and/or kinesthetic) as they directly experience and personally encounter oppression. In dealing with these situations, they must be able to notice oppressive behaviors, ideas, beliefs, values, feelings, and attitudes in themselves and others in their community and the social environment at large. Consequently, as they see, hear and otherwise experience oppression, they develop a sensory acuity and a heightened awareness that sharpens their perception and strengthens their observational skills.

Understandably, this sensory acuity and heightened awareness of oppression tends to be more developed in people with multiple subordinated identities, as they routinely witness and/or bear the brunt of oppressive incidents and conditions in multiple contexts. For instance, a black Puerto Rican lesbian is likely to be more aware of and alert to instances of oppression, as she personally must contend with dynamics of racism, colonialism, eurocentrism, sexism, and heterosexism on a daily basis as compared to a fair-skinned, male compatriot.

Furthermore, this heightened awareness tends to be more acute the further along the person is in her or his social identity development process; a person in the resistance stage is, generally, more perceptive of oppression than someone in the acceptance stage, while someone in the redefinition and internalization stages perceives more than a person in resistance. The cumulative knowledge gained from constant exposure to oppression also allows them to be increasingly aware of additional actions, more patterns and dynamics with ever greater subtlety and complexity. A person's attention becomes progressively more skillful, able to focus in on small details (e.g., tone of voice, eye movements, bodily tension) or zoom out onto larger patterns (e.g., Blacks routinely being followed in department stores; women regularly being ignored in male-led meetings; the relative success of light-skinned, straight-haired Latina/o crossover artists). While pattern recognition is a function of the next phase in the process (below), the examples here are used to point to the function of attention and our ability to intentionally shift it in various ways, a skill central to consciousness-in-action to be discussed later.

As mentioned earlier, as we become increasingly aware of oppression in the social environment, we also become increasingly aware of own internalized oppression as manifested through our own behaviors, ideas, beliefs, values, attitudes, and feelings. Our self-reflexive capacity, or more so, our skills of self-observation in the context of oppression will also become increasingly important to the process of consciousness-in-action.

Recognizing, Naming and Acknowledging

Enhanced awareness and the skills associated with attention greatly facilitate the second phase of the consciousness-in-action process: to **recognize, name,** and **acknowledge** instances and patterns of oppression. While throughout the social identity development process people naturally tend to discern specific patterns in the behaviors, ideas, beliefs, attitudes, etc., of others by social group (in addition to being instructed about these), during the process of consciousness-in-action a person intentionally directs attention to interactions, and seeks to recognize these as patterns that are predictable. For women, People of Color, gays, lesbians, bisexuals, transgendered people, and other groups who have historically endured violence because of their social identity, the ability to perceive, recognize and predict patterns of oppression generally tends to be a basic survival skill; they literally depend on the ability to recognize challenges and threats to their lives. Therefore, people who are regularly associated into their subordinated identities bring important recognition skills to the process, particularly if they are beyond the acceptance stage. And as men, whites, heterosexuals and other dominant group members also move past the passive acceptance stage of social identity development, they, too, become better skilled at perceiving and recognizing oppression, and may well find it more difficult to continue to ignore, deny, rationalize or minimize its presence and its impact (Hardiman and Jackson, 1997).

To acknowledge the existence of oppression and its impact moves us past our denial, a major characteristic of the acceptance stage, and into the resistance stage. To be able to admit to oneself and to others that injustices in the world are indeed related to the dynamics of oppression beyond their own doing is a major step, for dominant and subordinated members alike. To be able to name oppression as not merely a personal experience, but a shared reality is a tremendously important act of power in the process of consciousness-in-action toward liberation (Akbar, 1996; hooks, 2000b; Moane, 1999).

Similarly, it is an important step to be able to recognize the lack of harmony and acknowledge the cognitive dissonance within oneself and within the dominant culture previously presumed to be superior (Hardiman and Jackson, 1997). Recognition and acknowledgement of the contradictions and the lack of harmony motivate us to explore, to want to learn more, to further understand and make sense of this new level of cognitive awareness.

Understanding: Critical Analysis

The development of these abilities and skills does not automatically enable people to **understand** the complexity of oppression. It is necessary to develop the capacity for *critical analysis* through processes very much like those broadly used in social movements throughout the world: liberation pedagogy (Freire, 1970; McLaren and Leonard, 1993; Shor, 1992); theatre of the oppressed (Boal, 1985); liberation theology (Boff and Boff, 2004; Gutierrez, 1973/2005; McManus and Schlabach, 1991); liberation psychology (Hollander,

1997; Martín-Baró, 1994; Moane, 1999); community psychology (Montero, 2003, 2004; Nelson and Prilleltensky, 2005; Serrano-Garcia and Watts, 2003); feminism and feminist psychology (Herman, 1992; Moane, 2006; Mohanty, 2003); and the anti-oppression work of groups like The Four Worlds Development Project (Bopp et al., 1998), Highlander Research and Education Center (Horton and Freire, 1990), The People's Institute (Chisom and Washington, 1997), Crossroads Ministry, ilé, and so many others.

Understanding in the context of consciousness-in-action is about re-framing what we perceive and recognize, and ultimately, about assigning new meaning to what we have been socialized to believe. It is about questioning, re-examining, testing, and arriving at answers that actually explain the events, situations, conditions and patterns one observes and recognizes in oneself, in one of many identity groups, and in society as a whole. Understanding is also about considering historical causes, and in the process, uncovering and reclaiming more accurate versions of history than those offered by the dominant culture (Akbar, 1984, 1996; Martín-Baró, 1994).

Because of the spiraling and dynamic nature of the process, understanding loops back to support and strengthen one's perceptual and conceptual capacities, enhancing the ability to perceive, recognize and critically examine past and present realities. Furthermore, these enhanced capacities enable us to create and continually refine our vision of a desired future.

Together, our capacities to perceive (critical awareness), acknowledge (critical recognition) and understand (critical analysis) comprise what is otherwise known as *critical consciousness*. Yet critical consciousness is not sufficient to move us through the developmental process of liberation (Watts et al., 2003). Consciousness-in-action toward liberation, naturally, also requires action.

Responding: Moving to Intentional Action

As we begin to move from critical consciousness to action, we often continue to have emotional and behavioral reactions to oppression. Indeed, a broad range of reactions are considered stage-appropriate behaviors (Hardiman and Jackson, 1997), even if not entirely effective in obtaining results that lead to personal or collective goals. As mentioned in Chapter Three, confusion, doubt, pain, shame, guilt, fear, despair, powerlessness, helplessness, and hopelessness are common reactions for oppressed people at the acceptance stage, while frustration, anger, even rage are more typical of the resistance stage. Meanwhile, defensiveness, denial, and blaming are common reactions of dominant group members at the acceptance stage, while alienation, frustration, shame, guilt, anger toward, and attempt to distance themselves from, other members of their group(s) are appropriate to the resistance stage (1997).

Paradoxically, during the resistance stage, anger or rage can become an important and strategically useful source of personal power, enabling oppressed persons to express and assert themselves in ways in which they were previously unable. In this context, emotional reactions such as anger, rage or righteous indignation are signs of psychological healing, growth and development, as they can supply the motivating energy for personal change (Moane, 1999, 2003, 2006; Serrano-Garcia and Varas-Diaz, 2003). Meanwhile, collective anger and shared righteous indignation are also powerful motivators for, and instruments of, social and political action (Barbalet, 2001), such as the collective rage and indignation at the death of David Sanes, the Puerto Rican civilian guard killed by US Navy bombs, which re-kindled the decades old struggle for the demilitarization of Vieques.

However, reactive emotional states and behaviors eventually become a liability to the process of consciousness-in-action and, as such, become an obstacle to continued growth along the social identity development continuum. From a cognitive perspective, reactions are considered neuro-linguistically conditioned states that are unconsciously stimulated and automatically activated (Hall, 2000). In the context of oppression, reactive states leave persons who are subjectively associated into subordinated identities emotionally vulnerable and open to manipulation or exploitation, while they tend to leave persons associated into dominant identities feeling emotionally detached and inclined to act insensitively.

For example, anger and indignation are useful, if not instrumental, to anti-oppression organizing efforts, as they are, on the one hand, a sign that people have moved out of acceptance and into resistance, and, on the other, are a gauge of the emotional energy needed to carry out a long-term organizing strategy. However, anger and indignation usually do not come alone, but together with other expressions of emotional reactivity characteristic of the resistance stage: defensiveness, arrogance, disrespect, hostility, and other negative behaviors oppressed people tend to reproduce as they emulate dominant or oppressive patterns they have internalized. These reactions are particularly damaging to organizing efforts as they are often directed laterally at the very community being organized (Fanon, 1967; hooks, 1995; Memmi, 1965, 2000; Moane, 1999).

However, as we move into the redefinition and internalization stages of social identity development we push past our tendency to *react* and toward our ability to ***respond.***

A response, as defined in this framework, differs from a reaction in that a reaction is typically unconscious and automatic: "our buttons gets pushed," to use the popular expression. A response, on the other hand, is conscious and intended: it is a choice. When we respond, we tap into our inner resources and choose among those options available to us. These options will greatly depend on our critical consciousness, on what we have perceived, recognized, and understood about oppression in general, and about internalized inferiority and superiority, in others and ourselves.

Perhaps more than anything, the ability to respond relies on self-observation and our own transformation process. We are better able to transform that which we have understood; we are better able to understand that which we have recognized and acknowledged; we are better able to recognize and acknowledge that which we have perceived and observed.

To be pro-active, to act before a potentially harmful situation occurs, often seems beyond the reach of oppressed people, particularly those in communities confronting multiple and simultaneous oppressions. However, as we move into the redefinition and internalization stages of social identity development—and become more skilled at perceiving, recognizing and understanding—our ability to foresee potentially negative situations and access internal and external resources to take pre-emptive measures increasingly becomes another expression of response-ability. Not only might we imagine and create positive alternative options for resolving conflict and incongruities, we might also pro-actively envision desired goals for ourselves and alternative futures for our community.

There is no substitute for personal involvement in transforming reality, as active participation with one's own community of struggle is key to one's liberation (Bopp and Bopp, 2001; Martín-Baró, 1994; Moane, 1999). Meanwhile, courage, faith, solidarity, and commitment are among the traits that support the consistent acts of will throughout this active participation (Akbar, 1984, 1996).

As we develop our ability to respond, we integrate consciousness (perceive, recognize and understand) and will to act consciously and deliberately (vs. reacting unconsciously and impulsively). In so doing, we continue to resist the culture of imposition, continue to confront the dynamics of oppression, and seek and/or create alternatives that promote greater balance and harmony in the sphere of life.

Consciousness-in-Action throughout the Stages of Social Identity Development

As indicated throughout the chapter, the spiraling process of perceiving, recognizing, understanding and responding takes places at every stage along the social identity development continuum, from the naïve stage all the way through to the stage of internalization. As is illustrated in Figure 4.4, our successful cycling through perception, recognition, understanding, and responding to oppression within each developmental stage allows moving on to the next stage along the continuum. Like other developmental processes, all stages are essential to the overall process and no stage can be bypassed (Wilber, 2000a, 2000c, 2000d).

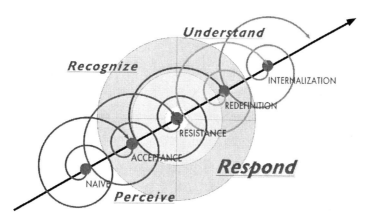

Figure 4.3: Movement through the Stages of Social Identity Development

However, since consciousness-in-action is the deliberate use of the functions of consciousness and will toward liberation, this process is not fully engaged until one moves from the acceptance stage into resistance.

Notwithstanding the absence of critical awareness and liberatory impulse in the naïve stage, a person at this stage is still engaged in a process of developing awareness of their social environment as she or he begins to internalize the belief system and social rules of the dominant culture. The primary developmental task of this stage, therefore, is to perceive differences among social groups and to begin to acquire the abilities and skills of perception previously described, abilities and skills that will continue to evolve.

As a person moves into the acceptance stage, their perception of difference evolves into the recognition and acknowledgement of these differences, albeit often named by people at this stage as discrimination. The ability to recognize and acknowledge, then, is the main developmental task of the acceptance stage. To re-cognize (to know again) and acknowledge (to admit to new knowledge) something perceived anew within one's field of awareness requires choice: an act of consciousness and will. This choosing to perceive, recognize and acknowledge, even if only to accept an oppressive reality or an ideology of supremacy in a specific social identity category, is the beginning of the process of consciousness-in-action.

During the resistance stage, the primary developmental task is to deepen understanding or critical analysis of these differential power dynamics as oppression. Meanwhile, as their perception, recognition, and understanding of external realities continue to evolve, people at this stage also develop greater critical consciousness and awareness of their own subjective experience, including their emotional reactivity. This prepares them for entry into the stage of redefinition.

The major developmental task of the redefinition stage is to overcome the emotional and behavioral reactivity of the resistance stage. While in resistance it is characteristic of a person to define her/himself in reactive opposition to the dominant social identity group (who s/he is not), in the re-definition stage she or he responds. In redefinition, a person consciously and deliberately claims and affirms who s/he is beyond internalized oppression and the external pressures to accommodate, collude, assimilate and be absorbed into the dominant cultural framework of a particular social identity.

The ability to respond carries into the internalization stage as a person integrates the new identity into the various aspects of life. From an integral and liberatory perspective, one of the most important challenges or tasks of this stage is to consciously and deliberately pursue development along all social identities, particularly those that are dominant. The abilities and skills of perception, recognition, critical under-standing, and response-ability are also integrated as they con-tinue to evolve into higher levels of pro-activity, liberated creativity, and transformative action.

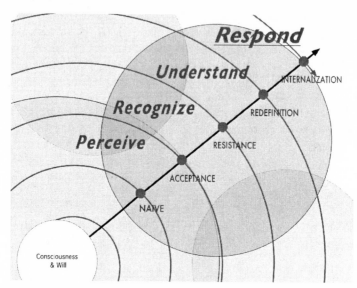

Figure 4.4: Developmental Tasks throughout Social Identity Development

From Reactivity to Response-ability

The process of consciousness-in-action is supported by virtually any activity or process, individual and collective, that engages and further develops our perception, recognition, and understanding of our oppressed condition. Some of these will be discussed in the following chapter. Yet, developing the ability to respond is perhaps the most significant challenge in the process of consciousness-in-action as we move along the stages of social identity development.

From this integral liberation perspective, to respond is not so much to have the ability to control or subdue the reactive emotions, limiting frames and negative behaviors internalized during socialization in the culture of oppression. To respond is, in effect, to transcend—to embrace yet move beyond—our reactions, as we may always feel the pain, shame, fear, and anger that arises in us in the presence of oppression. And while feeling the feelings that arise, it is still possible to tap into our abilities to perceive, recognize, and understand from ever-broader and varied perspectives, and deliberately choose an effective course of action. Then, to choose and carry out that action—despite our socially conditioned internalized inferiority or superiority—becomes an act of authentic power, a sign of personal liberation, and an expression of a transformed self.

However, transcending internalized oppression, thus overcoming the tendency to react, is no small developmental task. Even after we have acquired the sensory acuity, knowledge and insight sufficient to catch ourselves, in the moment, with a defensive attitude and while feeling self-contracted, we may still find it difficult to break the patterned emotional state. Or even when at times of extreme tension we notice that our focus is fixated and our perspective is narrow (a literal experience of tunnel vision), we may still find it almost impossible to shift the perceptual frames to which we have been conditioned, into which we automatically—unconsciously—associate. Taking these emotional states and perceptual frames into consideration, it is not surprising that we, then, continue to replicate the conditioned reactive behaviors, or defenses, we have internalized.

This cycle of reactivity itself becomes an obstacle to movement to the next stage of development within the larger process of liberation. And while we do not lose the abilities or faculties accumulated throughout the previous stages in our process, our inability to respond in ways appropriate to that particular stage keeps us looping back into perceiving-recognizing-understanding phases of the consciousness-in-action cycle. Therefore, the ability to respond represents a key juncture at each stage, a gateway of sorts to the subsequent stage of development. See Figure 4.5 below.

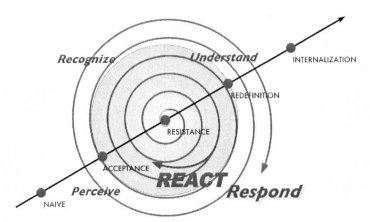

Figure 4.5: Response and Reaction in Social Identity Development Process

Overcoming the tendency to react, therefore, is central to the process of liberation and to continued development. However, the ability to interrupt conditioned patterns, and eventually transcend internalized oppression, depends on the capacity for self-observation and skill at utilizing various subjective faculties available to us.

Building upon our sensory acuity or heightened awareness of events, patterns and dynamics in the social environment, our movement toward response-ability develops as we become skillful in managing or utilizing our subjective experience by controlling emotional states, shifting perceptual positions, re-orienting in time, and quieting the mind.

Controlling Emotional States

Awareness, understanding and, eventually, control over our emotional states are fundamental in developing our ability to respond. In a society where people, as children, are routinely trained, often through severe punishment, to suppress, repress or otherwise ignore very basic emotions—boys their fear and sadness, girls their anger—it is not surprising that as adults we may not be particularly skilled at recognizing or acknowledging our emotional states. Therefore, to increase our likelihood of moving beyond reaction and into response, it is important to become aware of our state of reactivity. Further, it is important to develop consciousness (perception, recognition and understanding) of the fear, anger, hate, defensiveness, numbness and wide range of emotions that surface in the context of oppression as presented in Chapter 3.

Paradoxically, focusing our attention on these reactive feelings facilitates the process of breaking our states of emotional reactivity. This process involves examining what it is we are feeling. Further, the process can be advanced if we closely examine just how we subjectively experience and visually, auditorily and/or kinesthetically represent and, then, name these reactions, as for example, the knot in the stomach as anger; a tightness in the chest and shallow breath as fear; an ache in the heart as sadness; tunnel vision and a racing heart as anxiety; a clouded mind and scattered thoughts as confusion; a critical parental voice in the left ear as guilt; a burning sensation of the face and ears as shame. There can be any number of combinations. As our emotional intelligence deepens, we become better able to observe, recognize and understand the particular patterns of emotional reactivity: the vulnerabilities we have developed; the words, behaviors, actions, etc., and contexts that trigger them; the frequency, intensity, and duration of these reactive feelings; the usual behaviors resulting from these particular feelings.

Overall, emotional reactivity is accompanied by a sense of self-contraction and separateness from others. This sense of separateness, both in terms of perceived separation and a feeling of emotional distance, has direct bearing on our perspective: from where we view ourselves and our circumstance (either particular or general) in relation to the other person(s) in a given differential power dynamic, to the social group(s) with which we identify, to the community to which we belong, to our society and its institutions, and to humanity and the Divine at large. The more angry or fearful we feel in relation to another, the group, the community and/or the world, the more contracted, individuated, isolated, separate we will feel. And in this reactive state, our attention is directed inward, turned away from others and, thus, blind to what is occurring beyond the self and, often, even blind to the self. Therefore, breaking the emotional state of reactivity also enables us to turn attention toward all aspects of the self and outward in more expansive views or perspectives.

Shifting Perceptual Positions

In this context, the ability to shift our perspective or point of view between various perceptual positions within a system becomes an important skill (Bodenhamer and Hall, 2000; Dilts, 1996; O'Connor, 1998). A concept from NLP, perceptual positions refers to a model describing three to five different perspectives a person can subjectively assume from which to observe phenomena and the world (Merlevede, Bridoux, and Vandamme, 2001).

Applied to the integral liberation framework, *first position* refers to an interaction or relationship as seen from the point of view of the individual, the "I." From this perspective, we see ourselves and the interaction out of our own eyes, so to speak, on the basis of our particular frames of reference, e.g., ideas, behaviors, attitudes, beliefs, feelings and values, and, of course, our social identities and differential power status.

Second position refers to the point of view of the other person(s) in an interaction, together with their frames of references. More precisely, to assume second position *does not* mean that we adopt the other person's point of view. Rather, it means that we momentarily imagine that we perceive, recognize and understand the interaction or situation, and even ourselves, as if from the perspective of that other person on the basis of *their* worldview: to see as they see, to think as they think, to understand what they value, to feel as they feel (Merlevede, et al., 2001; O'Connor, 1998). It is safe to say that if we are in a reactive emotional state, we run the risk of projecting what we fear they might see, think, believe, or feel, especially about us. However, if we are coming from a more responsive emotional state, second position we may lead us toward true empathy.

Third position is the perspective of the detached outside observer, a vantage point from which we are able to observe our self, the other person(s) and the dynamics of the relationship. Within this integral liberation framework, third position also refers to the perspective of one's social identity group(s), as this perspective ideally represents the imagined critical observations of someone at the internalization stage of social identity development. This perspective might be evoked from asking oneself, "What would my mentor say about this situation, what would she see that I don't see from either first position or second position?" This can be helpful to the extent that we have accurate internal representations of individuals at that level.

Fourth position refers to a system-wide perspective, for instance, from the imagined point of view of an organization at a given moment (O'Connor, 1998).[17] From the perspective of this model, fourth position also represents the viewpoint of our community as internally represented. This could be our geographic community, our community-of-

---

[17] O'Connor views the first four perceptual positions at snapshots a given moment in time, with the fifth position being the system's view (fourth position) seen over time. From the integral perspective, perceptual positions are necessarily historical in nature.

struggle, or a particular organization to which we are accountable. This is a vantage point from which not only the interaction is viewed, but so are other community members, historical dynamics and patterns, and the potential impacts of the interaction within the larger system or community. It is also a place from which we can tap into (or remind ourselves of) ancestral knowledge and wisdom. An organizer or community leader, for example, might ask herself, "How is my behavior likely to be perceived by my community-of-struggle in terms of our shared values, desired goals and collective vision? What would our community elders and those that have past and those yet to be born have to say about me and/or this course of action?"

Meanwhile, *fifth position* refers to increasingly more expansive points of view, ranging from an entire society, a hemisphere, humanity as a whole, the planet's ecosystem, higher spiritual realms, to The Great Nest of Being itself. From this perspective, questions like "How will this action be viewed ten or twenty years from now?" can surely lead to deep reflection and contemplation.

The ability to consciously and effectively shift perceptual position (versus engage in projection) requires a break from reactive emotional states. Additionally, as this ability to shift to more expansive perceptual positions is sequential and cumulative (second requires and includes first, third requires and includes second and first, and so on), seeing the present situation from multiple perspectives allows for the possibility of both deeper critical understanding and a broader range of options to respond.

Orientation in Time

Another aspect of subjective experience that may be useful in moving from reaction to response is the ability to bring attention to **orientation in time** and shift it if and when necessary.

When orientation in time is in the present, we tend to focus on current conditions, presenting problems, negative impacts or symptoms, particularly when addressing issues of oppression. When time orientation points toward the past, we tend to focus on historical antecedents and causes for today's situations. When oriented toward the future, attention tends to focus on seeking solutions, identifying desired outcomes, on articulating a vision yet to come. From an integral perspective, all time orientations are equally important, and are essential to the process of developing critical consciousness toward liberation.

Yet, when we are in a reactive state the tendency is to become fixated in a particular time orientation. From a present time orientation, problems that arise seem personal, pervasive, and permanent; we find it difficult to analyze root causes, identify potential resources, or explore possible solutions. From a past time orientation, current problems carry the weight of history and feel overwhelming and insurmountable, giving raise to expressions such as "Things have always been that way and will always be." Meanwhile, from a future time orientation fixated by emotional reactivity, we tend to focus attention on possible solutions without having thoroughly assessed the present situation nor considered its causes. Additionally, one's feelings and those of others involved tend to be dismissed or ignored, as if to avoid their full impact.

Therefore, developing greater awareness of preferred time orientation, particularly while in reactive states, and becoming skillful at shifting to include all orientations in time can foster and enhance the process of responding.

Quieting the Mind

Lastly, the ability to respond can be further developed through practices and disciplines that direct intentionality toward quieting the mind, or bypass inner dialogues, images, feelings and other internal representations, and move us closer to unmediated perception and direct experience. This can be achieved (or approximated) through activities such as meditation, prayer, physical exercise, contemplation of nature, or music. While it may not be possible or practical to sit in meditation or go for a run in all settings where reactivity might arise, it is possible to effectively engage in certain aspects of these practices, e.g., focused breathing, a silent mantra, or a relaxation technique, or otherwise elicit more responsive states and effective perceptual frames recalled from previous experiences of quietude or flow.

The act of intentionally bringing attention to reactive states and limiting frames, like noticing serious physiological symptoms or observing sociological conditions, is in itself the beginning of the release of contraction, of the healing process, of resolution of problems. The intentional and skilled use of attention, then, not only breaks the reactivity in the moment, but also begins to interrupt the psychological pattern of internalized oppression. In turn, this release may open the path to more responsive alternatives, to a greater sense of connection to self and others, and advancement of the overall process of liberation and social transformation.

Closing Comments

With this chapter, I have sought to present consciousness-in-action as a process that occurs within each stage of social identity development and across the stages along a continuum. Moreover, I have sought to present an integral perspective that addresses social identity as a core aspect of human development, as important as the multiple developmental lines so thoroughly researched by integral theorists (Combs, 2002; Wilber, 1999), e.g., the emotional (Goleman, 1995), cognitive (Kegan, 1982), self (Loevinger, 1976), value systems (Beck and Cowan, 1996; Graves, 2002), moral

(Gilligan, 1993), spiritual (Wilber, 1999e, 2000d), needs (Maslow, 1968, 1971), among others. Certainly, from a liberation psychology perspective, social identity development along its multiple developmental lines—race, class, gender, culture, nationality, sexuality, religion, political ideology, age, and ability—is central and essential.

I also want to point out that in this discussion I have deliberately focused on aspects of the subjective experience of the process of consciousness-in-action, as this area has been largely overlooked in the literature on liberation psychology and related fields. Conversely, while this area is within the domain of neuro-linguistic programming, its application to liberation processes appears to have been virtually ignored.

In the following chapter, I present the framework and the process of consciousness-in-action as an integral approach to change that extends beyond the individual.

Chapter 5
An Approach to Integral Change

The pedagogy of the oppressed, as a humanist and libertarian pedagogy, has two distinct stages. In the first, the oppressed unveil the world of oppression and through the praxis commit themselves to its transformation. In the second, in which the reality of oppression has already been transformed, this pedagogy ceases to belong to the oppressed and becomes a pedagogy of all people in the process of permanent liberation. In both stages, it is always through action in depth that the culture of domination is culturally confronted.

Paulo Freire
Pedagogy of the Oppressed
(1970/2005, p.54)

In Chapter 4, I focused on the process of consciousness-in-action primarily from a liberation perspective. From this perspective, consciousness-in-action is about disrupting patterns of internalized oppression—both internalized inferiority and superiority—by overcoming reactive states and transcending limiting frames so that responsive action against institutional oppression may be taken.

Yet, at the same time that consciousness-in-action is concerned with the liberation of people from oppression within and without, it is also concerned with the transformation of self and others in ways that foster the evolution of human consciousness and the emergence of a new society. Here, in the final chapter of this book, I extend the framework to propose an integral change approach that is both liberatory and transformative, an approach that is based on practice and application in both personal and social spheres, and that is oriented toward change in both dimensions. As examples, I offer brief descriptions of two efforts with which I am

familiar that, to varying degrees, embody integral approaches
to personal and social change.

Integral Change Approach

In societies where repressive institutions and oppressive cultural paradigms are pervasive, it is not surprising that those
societies would generate collective resistance, albeit reactive,
and liberatory approaches among its oppressed populations.
These liberation approaches, in turn, incorporate various
methodologies of the oppressed (Sandoval, 2000; Smith,
1999) that reflect the stages of collective identity development of their societies.

      Approaches, such as liberation pedagogy (Freire,
1970; Horton and Freire, 1990; Shor, 1992), liberation theology (Boff and Boff, 2004; Gutierrez, 1973/2005; McManus
and Schlabach, 1991), liberation spirituality (Eppsteiner,
1988; Sivaraksa, 1992), liberation ethics (Dussel,
1998/2000), liberation psychology (Bulhan, 1985; Fanon,
1963, 1967; Moane, 1999), tend to emphasize past and external (objective) conditions, circumstances, obstacles and challenges in the collective dimension. These and specific liberation practices, among which are participatory action research
(Nelson and Prilleltensky, 2005), theatre of the oppressed
(Boal, 1985), study circles, consciousness-raising and support
groups, kitchen-table counseling (hooks, 1993), community
organizing (Hope and Timmel, 1999), protest rallies and
marches, strikes, boycotts, and non-violent civil disobedience, (Ferris and Sandoval, 1997; Martinez, 1991; Sivaraksa,
1992), and the psychological treatment of the trauma of oppression (Herman, 1992; Hollander, 1997; Root, 1992;
Wineman, 2003), often aspire to mitigate the negative effects
of oppression and, moreover, eradicate their historical causes.
In so doing, they seek to account for and remedy past abuses
and neglect, correct distortions and misrepresentations of history, heal the collective psychic wounds inflicted, reclaim

cultural heritage either lost or taken away, and restore personal pride and collective dignity (Akbar, 1984, 1996; hooks, 1993; Martín-Baró, 1994).

Meanwhile, approaches that could be considered transformative, and utilize techniques such as creative visualization, exercise, meditation, and ritual (Arrien, 1993; Hart, 1987; Houston, 1982, 2000; Leonard and Murphy, 1995), neurolinguistic and accelerated learning approaches (Bandler, 1992a; Lankton, 1980; O'Connor, 1998; Rose, 1985), and transpersonal psychotherapies (Assagioli, 1965/1976; Deikman, 1982; Firman and Gila, 2002; Tart, 1992) tend to emphasize present and internal (subjective) realities as they affect the individual. These approaches and practices also tend to emphasize the transcendence of personal patterns to allow for the emergence of inner qualities that, in turn, generate opportunities for improved subjective and objective conditions in the future. Among those that seek to extend personal growth methodologies to the collective dimension are organizational transformation (Covey, 1990; Fisher, 2000; Scharmer, 2004; Stanfield, 2000), spiritual activism (Adair, 2001, 2003; Horwitz, 2002; Nhat Hanh, 1992), and Spiral Dynamics (Beck and Cowan, 1996; Graves, 2002; Wilber, 2000a).

So, while liberation could be characterized as the *struggle against* oppression, transformation could be characterized as the *movement toward* a future vision. Yet, from the perspective of this integral framework, liberation and transformation are not approaches in opposition to each other. Instead, they are complementary forces for change. Both liberation and transformation approaches are essential to the developmental process of integral well-being, and as such, they are bound to, and contained within, each other (Prilleltensky, 2003).

Without this integration, efforts for change would likely fluctuate between reactive attempts to dismantle oppression (including revolutionary change that merely seeks to invert the dominant-subordinated power dynamic), and efforts to manipulate subjectivities that hope to bring into being a new era (including liberal reforms that essentially leave structural inequities and supremacist ideologies intact). A synergy created by the full embrace of both liberatory and transformative approaches is needed to move people—individually and collectively—to higher stages of human development.

Representing the integration of these complementary forces, Figure 5.1 (below) illustrates many of the key elements of an integral change approach to liberation and transformation. At the center of the figure is the sphere of human activity and being within the context of the cyclone of oppression and matrix of domination. This central sphere is situated in the present along the time continuum, a position from which historical causes of the current situation can be critically analyzed and from which a future of desired outcomes can be envisioned. From this place and time, both internal challenges and external obstacles can be assessed. It is also from the perspective of this time and circumstance that both internal resources and external opportunities for change can be appropriately identified and strategically accessed. From this center, the process of consciousness-in-action is set into spiraling motion, perceiving, recognizing, understanding and resisting oppression while generating liberatory-transformative responses at intrapersonal, interpersonal, community and systemic levels.

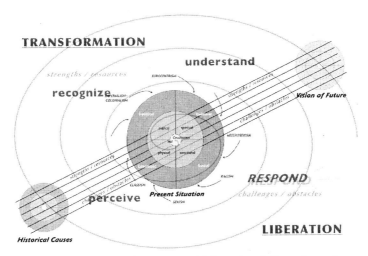

TRANSFORMATION

understand

recognize

Vision of Future

RESPOND

perceive   Present Situation

LIBERATION

Historical Causes

Figure 5.1: Integral Change toward Liberation & Transformation

Integral Practice for Integral Change

As already established, any integrated approach to integral change requires processes that are simultaneously individual and collective, subjective and objective. These approaches would need to foster the emergence of ever-higher developmental stages along multiple lines in all aspects of being and human activity while also actively challenging current manifestations of institutional and internalized oppression. The creation of actual integral change approaches to individual and collective well-being that is simultaneously liberatory and transformative presents a formidable challenge.

Given this challenge, transformative strategies to personal growth may well prove to be resources worthy of consideration. Developed within the human potential movement of the 1960s and 70s, and from transpersonal psychology and new age movements of the 1980s and 90s, various transformative practices were adopted and adapted from ancient indigenous spiritual and cultural traditions from around the world. George Leonard and Michael Murphy, pioneers in these movements, developed what they call *integral transformative practice,* a comprehensive strategy embracing many of these approaches (1995). Based on the premise that "lasting transformation requires long-term practice" (p.16), Leonard and Murphy describe *integral transformative practice* as a program of long-term disciplined activities aimed at creating positive changes in the body (e.g., diet, exercise, martial arts training), mind (e.g., reading, study, discussion), heart (e.g., support groups, community involvement), and soul (e.g., meditation, yoga).

Like Leonard and Murphy's notion of integral transformative practice, an integral change approach would require long-term, regular, and disciplined effort in order to develop capacities that enhance the processes of consciousness-in-action and social identity development. Integral practices, then, would include the exercise of consciousness and will as applied to the physical, mental, spiritual and emotional aspects of the self. Physical exercise, healthy diet, and stress reduction practices would be particularly important to people working in communities-of-struggle given the many ways oppression negatively impacts them. Meditation can be especially useful to the process of perceiving and recognizing patterned reactions that, in addition to nurturing and supporting one's spiritual development, is very useful in moving toward responsive action in social contexts.

Spheres of Action, Spheres of Influence

Such integral change approaches would also need to be simultaneously personal and communal, involving individuals, groups, communities, and/or organizations engaging and mutually influencing each other. As tends to occur in collective processes, the person's level of engagement expands from passive to increasingly active forms of participation (Bopp

and Bopp, 2001), and eventually from traditional, or patriar-
chal, leadership styles to shared, or feminist, leadership
(Kokopeli and Lakey, 1978). Along the way, a person's
sphere of influence also extends outward from the intrapersonal to the interpersonal, group, community, organizational
and institutional levels of the collective dimension (Bopp and
Bopp, 2001; Hope and Timmel, 1999; Moane, 2003). Initially, influence may be exercised among family members
and in time with other members of their particular identity
groups, communities-of-struggle, and/or within their larger
community. [See Figure 5.2.]

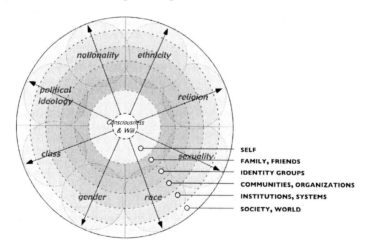

Figure 5.2: Spheres of Action and Influence

As a person continues to mature into the internalization stage of social identity development, they tend to generalize insights and lessons about one form of oppression to
other forms (Hardiman and Jackson, 1997). Therefore, for
instance, persons at this stage who are involved in anti-racism
work may also begin to address issues and dynamics of sex-

ism, heterosexism, colonialism and/or other forms of oppression within their current anti-racism networks. Alternatively (or additionally), they may extend their involvement to those other circles or networks, and eventually adopt a third world feminist perspective (Hill Collins, 2000; hooks, 2000b; Levins Morales, 2001; Mohanty, 2003) capable of grasping the intersections, distinctiveness, and commonalities of gender, race, culture, sexual, class, age, faith, and political oppressions and liberation struggles. In this way, on-going development of multiple social identities can both expand a person's leadership and deepen her/his influence on the collective.

In my community education and organizing work, for instance, the primary evidence of leadership development (in addition to observation and self-disclosure of subjective states and frames) is a person's ability to positively influence others in multiple and ever-expanding spheres of struggle. This influence, in turn, is evidenced by observable changes in the relational dynamics between them and others within and across social identities and differential power status that are indicative of advanced stages of social identity development and authentic power (degree of balance and harmony).

Regardless of stage of leadership or social identity development, however, change at the personal level is facilitated when linked to collective struggle as the person consciously, deliberately, and increasingly interacts with other people in their social environments regarding issues of social justice (Brewer and Hewstone, 2004; Freire, 1970; Moane, 2006; Stryker et al., 2000). Growth occurs *in* and *because of* relationship, particularly if these relationships are with others who are also engaged in consciousness-in-action, and are with people who can hold each other accountable to the values and principles inherent in liberation, transformation, and integral well-being. Accordingly, individuals are influenced by those within their sphere of action, if not for anything else, because their actions are reflected by those surrounding them. In this way, the person and others together can gauge the congruence between their intentions and their behaviors, as well as the degree of balance as they work toward shared desired outcomes.

Inward-Outward Spiraling Change

Much like community organizers who "educate, motivate, provide technical assistance, and give people a sense of their own power," functions prescribed by core trainers of The People's Institute's Undoing Racism/Community Organizing workshop, the work of integral change in community takes many forms and covers a lot of territory.

Beyond personal engagement in integral practices, a primary function of persons involved in integral change approaches is to *educate*. Integral change workers teach and provide accurate and corrective historical information to others within their spheres of influence that helps dismiss, dispel, dismantle, undermine, and reframe the disinformation, misinformation, stereotypes, and other distortions rooted in the culture of oppression (Akbar, 1984, 1996; Freire, 1970). More importantly, they seek to facilitate processes by which people can discover new knowledge that helps restore their self-image, self-concept, self-esteem and self-love, and gain insights that support their processes of consciousness-in-action (Leary, 2005; Martín-Baró, 1994).

New information, knowledge, and insight are also augmented by the on-going development of skills that support and further the work of liberation and transformation. In particular, integral change workers seek to learn and teach skills in managing subjective states and frames (such as those discussed in Chapter Four), human relations (e.g., communications, group dynamics, and process facilitation), and technologies relevant to their functions, roles, and desired outcomes.

Another mode of influencing integral change in others is by *inspiring and modeling*. Previously mentioned in Chapter 2, personal integrity, which arises out of increased balance and harmony, tends to be a source of inspiration for others, as people tend to look up to and imitate people they respect and admire. Personal integrity becomes a form of leadership to the extent that integral leaders model ways of being and doing, creating in others internal representations of that which they aspire to become. Teaching and leading by example is also instrumental in creating relationships and environments built on trust.

Indeed, *creating and sustaining relationship* is a vital function of an integral change worker. The demanding work of integral change requires a heart-felt sense of connection, of relationship based on reciprocity, solidarity, and camaraderie, and motivated by friendship, respect, love, and/or the realization of oneness. It is in the context of relationship that accountability among community members and commitment to struggle can be sustained.

And in the context of relationship, integral change workers *assist, support and work* with others engaged in liberatory-transformative action, some of whom are less advanced in their development as well as with some of who are further along. By accompanying others in community, integral change workers can facilitate processes that help disrupt automatic, often unconscious, patterns of internalized oppression.

In the process of educating, motivating, inspiring, modeling, relating, assisting, planning and taking action with others toward integral change, the personal and collective sense of possibility, hope, love and power of all involved is nurtured and sustained. These states of being are additionally fueled with compelling shared visions and with strategies that are in harmony and balance at individual, group, and community levels. Moreover, as other dynamic processes in this integral framework, these states, traits, and qualities, in turn, become sources of energy for on-going development along the path toward human well-being.

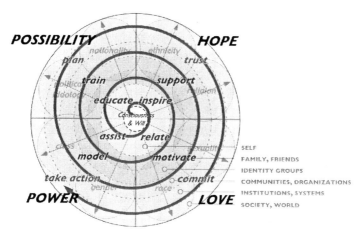

Figure 5.3: Integral Action in Community

Exemplars

The development and implementation of integral change approaches is a formidable task. Through ilé: Organizers for Consciousness-in-Action, staff members and associates[18] have been doing anti-oppression community organizing work in ways that approximate an integral approach or that, at least, apply many of its principles. The work of ilé also involves contact with a remarkable community institution, the St. Paul Community Baptist Church, which, without calling it integral change work, also appears to be guided by an integral vision and approach.

---

[18] ilé associates are people whom have participated in the organization's leadership development programs and community organizing efforts, and maintain a collaborative relationship with the organization toward advancing its goals.

Both St. Paul Community Baptist Church and ilé are briefly described in the following pages. These descriptions are not the result of formal research and evaluation processes, processes beyond the intended nature and scope of this study. Instead, the descriptions and analysis of both organizations are made on the basis of personal observation and engagement: with St. Paul's, as a guest and participant of church activities held in 1999 and 2000; with ilé, as its co-founder and co-director[19] from 1992 to 2005. Consequently, these descriptions are not intended as full and accurate representations of neither organization, its history, its current work, nor its effectiveness. My purpose here is to point to the two as examples of integral change approaches, that is, organizations that approach personal and collective liberation and transformation work from an integral perspective.

Saint Paul's Community Baptist Church

In mid-September 1999, and again one year later, I attended the event organized by the St. Paul Community Baptist Church, in Brooklyn, New York, known as The Commemoration of the *Maafa*. Each year since 1995, the staff and congregation of this African-American community church organizes a powerful series of workshops, lectures, worship, rituals, ceremonies, displays, theater, film, music, and community gathering — all "for the millions" lost in the *maafa*. *Maafa* is a Kiswahili term meaning "disaster" (Ani, 1980, p.12), "calamity, damage, injustice, misfortune, catastrophe" (Roberson, 1995, p.7), or the Black Holocaust (Anderson, 1995), and refers to "the great suffering of our people at the hands of Europeans in the Western hemisphere" (Ani, 1994,

---

[19] As co-director, co-founder and board member, I shared leadership in shaping ilé's vision and mission; as one of its original two educator-organizers, I also co-developed workshop and training curricula, co-facilitated workshops and training programs, and was directly involved in developing and implementing organizing strategies.

p.xxi). The Commemoration of the *Maafa* is not only a trib-
ute to the tens of millions of Africans who died between the
time of their capture, during the three-month trans-Atlantic
journey, or upon their arrival in the Americas (Roberson,
1995); the Commemoration of the *Maafa* is a carefully designed process of community healing of the intergenerational
trauma of internalized racial oppression of African peoples
(Leary, 2005).

    While Senior Pastor Rev. Dr. Johnny Ray
Youngblood, his staff, and the church's congregation may
well be unaware of integral theory or approaches, the Commemoration of the *Maafa*, as the work of St. Paul's in general, clearly falls within my definition of an integral approach
to human development.

    At the individual dimension, all aspects are addressed
by the activities and events held throughout the weeklong
commemoration. Of course, none of these activities can be
accurately described as addressing one aspect over another,
as these have positive impacts on all areas. For instance,
many of the lectures, workshops, presentations, exhibits of
historic artifacts, and Afrocentric and African affirming literature, are geared toward sharing information, knowledge
and wisdom, thus contributing to the **mental** development of
individual attendees, the congregation, the local community,
and of guests from across the US and other countries. Among
these events have been: The People's Institute's Undoing Racism workshop; Edwin Nichols' presentations on the *philosophical aspects of cultural difference* and skills for survival in a new world economy; pan-Africanist scholar Leonard Jeffries, Jr. on *pyramidal analysis*; neo-abolitionist author Noel Ignatiev on *How the Irish Became White* (1995);
Hong Sun Kang on Asian perspectives of racism in the US;
Robert Dilts, co-developer of NLP, on *The Healing Patterns
of Jesus* (1987); Na'im Akbar on *Breaking the Chains of
Psychological Slavery* (1984, 1996); Joy Leary on *Post-*

Traumatic Slavery Syndrome (2005); Santería priestess and author Marta Moreno-Vega on aspects of the African diaspora in the Caribbean (2000). While these activities are oriented primarily to deeper participants' understanding, they also significantly contribute to the psychological or **emotional** healing of those in attendance.

Participants' **spiritual** development is also supported through worship services, ritual, and a sweat lodge, as well as various forms of artistic expression. Prominent among these activities have included: Pastor Youngblood's inspired and inspiring worship services; *The Maafa Suite,* a master performance-ceremony; the church's gospel choir; and, the *Firewalk,* a collective psycho-spiritual-empowerment ritual ceremony led by NLP master practitioner, Jeffrey Vincent Noble. Through these events, participants, particularly through *The Maafa Suite* and the *Firewalk,* also engage the **physical** aspect, while also experiencing emotional healing, mental awakening, and spiritual nourishment.

The activities and experiences of the *maafa* commemoration process also support the development of **psychosocial aspects** (self-image, self-concept, self-esteem, and self-love) at both individual and collective levels. Done from an explicitly anti-racist perspective, these experiences are designed to counteract psychological manifestations of internalized racial inferiority of St. Paul's primarily African American congregation, and to support social identity development from the resistance through internalization stages.

While the activities are developed primarily for African Americans, they are certainly relevant to Latinos/as and other People of Color regardless of their African ancestry. Furthermore, white anti-racism participants report that the events helped them —intellectually, psychologically and spiritually— in their struggle to heal, transcend, and develop beyond their internalized racial superiority.

The **political, cultural** and **social** aspects of the collective dimension are also addressed through many of the same events, as they all served to bring people of African descent together in a variety of ways in order for them to embrace their history and affirm their culture, fostering a greater sense of power as a community. This is also done taking into account **economic** considerations, as financial resources of the congregation and guests are used to support Black-owned businesses and talent in the local community, and to hire Black experts from other parts of the country.

In addition to yearly special events like the *Commemoration of the Maafa*, St. Paul Community Baptist Church also runs its own elementary school and educational programs for young and old throughout the year. The church has provided and/or paid for training and professional development opportunities, including certification in NLP, for many of its staff, elders, and parishioners. Also, a bookstore stocks an excellent selection of African American and Afrocentric literature on a wide range of subjects, simultaneously providing learning and cultural affirmation for readers of all ages, and contributing to economic self-sufficiency of the church.

Even beyond its congregation, St. Paul Community Baptist Church is a force with which to contend in the African American community of East New York. Locally, the church has confronted community problems that include drug related crime, violence, housing, economic development, as well as a host of issues that directly impact congregation members and their families. Nationally, Rev. Youngblood's church brought together the largest concentration of participants to the Million Man March, second only to its principle convener, the Nation of Islam's Minister Louis Farrakhan himself. The work of Pastor Youngblood and St. Paul's is featured in an award winning book, *Upon This Rock: The Miracles of a Black Church* (Freedman, 1993).

With the development of the *Commemoration of the Maafa*, now shared with other communities across the US, and the church's various ministries in service of its congregation and larger community, their work has evolved into an exemplar of an integral liberatory-transformative approach.

ilé: Organizers for Consciousness-in-Action

Founded in 1992 as the Institute for Latino Empowerment, ilé: Organizers for Consciousness-in-Action was conceived as a Latino antiracism education and leadership development program. Its work was inspired by The Four Worlds' medicine wheel (Bopp et al., 1989), liberation pedagogy (Freire, 1970; Hope and Timmel, 1984; Shor, 1992), social justice education models (Hardiman and Jackson, 1997; Lester and Johnson, 1990), and most importantly, the work of the Latino Empowerment Education Circle. Over its fifteen-year history, ilé's work has continued evolved into an integral approach to organizing for liberation and transformation.

ilé's stated mission is to advance "anti-oppression community organizing and Latino/a leadership development in the US and Puerto Rico. We work to create systemic and institutional changes that may lead to people's liberation from racism, classism, sexism, militarism, imperialism, and other forms of oppression" (www.conciencia-en-accion.org). As active participant/leaders in a larger social movement, ilé's goals are: "to develop, support, and strengthen the leadership of Latinos/as who struggle against oppression in their communities; to promote integral community organizing as a key process for collective development and self-determination within Latino communities; and to facilitate effective collaborations, both among Latinos/as, and between Latinos/as and African Americans, Native Americans, Asian Americans, whites, and others also committed to social transformation" (ibid).

Based in Puerto Rico since 1997, most of its work is carried on within the many struggles in this US colony. In the US, the work focuses on racism as a rallying point for Latino/a leadership development and multiracial community development. In both contexts, ilé's efforts use an integral approach to organizing (see Figure 5.3) as its core methodology that is designed to educate, motivate, inspire, model, assist and/or support individuals, groups and organizations in ways that enhance their sense of power and collective purpose.

While ilé's organizing efforts are directed against oppression, its processes center on the transformation of people through **consciousness-in-action**. Whether the issue of engagement is racism, eurocentrism, militarism, imperialism, sexism, classism, heterosexism, ageism, or ableism, ilé's efforts simultaneously seek to help people perceive, recognize, and take responsive action based on understanding that:

- oppression in all its forms is the root cause of today's problems and circumstances, that all of its various forms are interconnected and interdependent, and all forms must be understood and addressed;
- institutional and internalized oppression work hand in hand to keep people from organizing to work for change, and that one cannot be changed without change of the other;
- liberation and transformation of society can occur only as a result of the organized efforts of a movement of people capable of living social justice and who are personally committed to the restoration of our full humanity, and;
- people collectively already have the resources necessary for (re)establishing integral well-being and moving toward full development in all aspects and dimensions, and have the capacity to take positive action now.

Over the past fifteen years, ilé has developed and implemented a wide range of efforts to train and organize people, most of whom are Latinas/os. These efforts include: workshops and leadership training programs; psycho-educational counseling and leadership coaching; study circles and healing circles; group facilitations and organizational development interventions; local, national and international organizing meetings; social and cultural events; public speaking engagements and media campaigns; published articles and other written materials; protest demonstrations and civil disobedience actions.

Different aspects of the integral approach through consciousness-in-action are emphasized in the various efforts. For instance, the primary purpose of the workshops (e.g., *Pa'lante Unidos: Latinos/as Together Against Racism, Rompiendo esquemas raciales,* Don't be eRACEd by the Census) is to create critical consciousness about racism and its impact on Latino well-being and development while simultaneously planting seeds for future community organizing (Quiñones Rosado, 1998; 2000; 2002a; 2002b; Reinat Pumarejo, 2005). Participants are introduced to many of the concepts and conceptual maps of the integral change framework, e.g., integral well-being, institutional oppression, internalized superiority and inferiority, consciousness-in-action, and integral organizing. Through dialogical processes they describe present conditions (**perceive**), acknowledge patterns (**recognize**), and engage in critical analysis (**understand**) of historical causes and on-going sociological dynamics that give rise to the realities they experience as people that live, work and/or are otherwise connected to Latino community. These processes examine impacts of oppression on all aspects of both individual and the collective dimensions. In considering the process of consciousness-in-action, participants are encouraged to consider personal and community resources available to them as they seek to **respond**, including aspects of their culture(s) that can be utilized and/or reclaimed.

ilé's leadership development training efforts, Latino Leaders Program and, more recently, *Programa de Organizadores Comunitarios*, build on concepts, information, and processes addressed in the workshops, and on participants' experience in community struggle. The main goal of training programs is to help participants, specifically people involved in community organizing and/or organizational leadership roles, increase capacity for consciousness-in-action. To this end, the training processes are geared to hone skills for interpersonal communications, group facilitation, and development of strategic interventions. Equally important, the training program addresses specific issues of internalized oppression that lead to emotional reactivity and it explores ways of interrupting these reactive patterns and replacing them with responsive behaviors. More so than in the workshops, the importance of community (particularly concerning genuine connection with and mutual support among members) and the power of culture (especially the values of committed relationship together with shared vision, shared leadership, and shared responsibility) are emphasized. Oppressive aspects of Latin American (and other) cultures that undermine liberating and transformative organizing are also examined and critiqued, principally those related to colonial manifestations of racism, colorism[20], sexism, homophobia, classism, and other forms of oppression.

Psycho-educational support is also available to current and past participants individually. Interventions may include therapeutic counseling, goal-oriented coaching, instruction in stress management and meditation, and/or application

---

[20] A manifestation of internalized racism among People of Color and racially mixed cultures which contextually privileges lighter-skinned members and further penalizes darker-skinned members, particularly (in Latin American cultures) those who are notably Afro-descendant.

of Reiki traditional healing. All of these processes, however, are culturally contextualized and done within an integral anti-oppressive transformative perspective. These are explicitly geared to further support participants' effective dealing with reactivity stemming from internalized inferiority and/or superiority that is manifested within the physical, mental, spiritual and/or emotional aspects of the self, for the most part as they relate to patterns present within the family, at work, school, or elsewhere within their broader sphere of activity and influence. Much of this psycho-educational work, as in the leadership training program, is based on the participant's integral self-assessment of internal and external obstacles as well as resources. The creation or reinforcement of external support systems, whether it consists of one person or an entire network (or community) of people, is a fundamental aspect of this personal level work.

About once each year, ilé organizes and facilitates an event that brings together anti-oppression training, leadership development, and community organizing with collective healing and cultural affirmation. Among such efforts, *África en mi piel, África en mi ser* (Africa on my Skin, Africa in my Soul) stands out as a prime example of an integral approach. *África en mi piel* is a synergistic women's empowerment, leadership, and organizing project in response to cultural racism and sexism in Puerto Rico. Over a two- to three-month period, Puerto Rican women—regardless of age, education, class background, and phenotype—are engaged in a series of activities and processes that foster their social identity development as women of the African diaspora. Participants are involved in dialogues, workshops, healing circles, planning meetings, working sessions, rehearsals and production of the project's culminating act: a two-hour illustrative workshop/performance in African and Afro-Puerto Rican history and culture through textiles, symbols, fashion design, music and movement before an audience of community members.

As an integral approach, these processes involve the **mental, physical, spiritual, and emotional** aspects of the individual (participants and the community/audience), while also involving the **political, economic, cultural, and social** aspects in all phases of design and implementation of the project.

These processes are liberatory as they address issues related to what it means to be a woman in Puerto Rico. Through these processes, institutional and internalized racism, and its connection with culture, gender, and Puerto Rico's colonial relationship to the US and its racial paradigm, are thoroughly explored by all participants. These processes are also transformative as, throughout, the women are reframing, reaffirming, and/or otherwise enhancing their individual and collective **self-image, self-concept, self-worth, and self-love**. Simultaneously, their roles in relationship to each other and their community tend to shift along the observer-participant-leader continuum, particularly as their influence extends beyond the group of women as well as the duration of the project.

África en mi piel is an excellent example of integral organizing as it brings together women, who might not otherwise be connected, on a topic that they might not otherwise address. Moreover, the project succeeds at bringing together people from communities who also might not otherwise gather to observe, participate and share with the participants, nor with each other, in recognition and celebration of their Africanness—no small feat given the historical context of racism in Puerto Rico and it persistent and insidious nature.

In 2004, *África en mi piel, África en mi ser* was held in Vieques at the request of *Alianza de Mujeres Viequenses*, a local women's organization, based on on-going relationships built during ilé's active involvement in the struggle to expel the US Navy. From 1999 through 2003, the whole spectrum of ilé's integral approach was utilized, from training, coaching, and process facilitation to fundraising, grantwriting, and organizing public support. Moreover, grounded in the principle that the personal is political and the political is personal, ilé co-directors personally organized and participated in acts of civil disobedience, resulting in their arrest, conviction and incarceration. In confinement and upon their release, they continued to do their organizing and healing work among other detainees and, primarily, with Vieques community leaders and members in the movement—including *Alianza de Mujeres Viequenses* and other groups.

While ilé's work is principally in Puerto Rico and within Latino communities in the US, for the past ten years it has also worked closely with other organizations and communities in its anti-oppression organizing and movement building, including in other countries. ilé has been invited to join organizing efforts with PeaceWatch in Northern Ireland, the East Asia/Puerto Rico/US Women Against Militarism Network in Japan, Okinawa and South Korea, and with The People's Institute for Survival & Beyond in Soweto, South Africa. The organizing work of ilé co-founder and co-director, María I. Reinat-Pumarejo, has been recognized internationally with inclusion among the 1000 Women for the Nobel Peace Prize collectively nominated in 2005.

Other Observations

Both ilé and St. Paul's hold a multidimensional vision of human activity and a deep commitment to transform individuals and society. Both organizations are guided by an integral view and a strategy of cohesive activities and processes that foster and support well-being, empowerment, and on-going development through liberatory and transformative actions that address all aspects, all dimensions, and all stages of life.

It is also true that each of them approaches integral change work from their own ethnocentric perspectives: ilé with its Latino-centric view, and St. Paul's, an Afrocentric approach. While the racial and cultural specificity of these particular orientations might lead Wilber and other observers to take exception to my assessment of ilé and St. Paul's approach as integral,[21] I would argue that St. Paul's decidedly Afrocentric approach and ilé's Latino-centric orientation are conscious *responses* (not unconscious reactions) to the egocentric and ethnocentric worldviews of the dominant white culture. These ethnocentric approaches are not only necessary for the African American and Latino communities served; these are developmentally appropriate strategies that serve the community at large as part of a broad anti-racist, anti-oppression movement toward a world-centric or integral worldview and social transformation.

Undoubtedly, both organizations upon closer examination would reveal challenges or inconsistencies related to this integral change approach. Being intimately familiar with ilé, I could readily point to numerous (and persistent) challenges to the principles and practice of integral change at multiple levels: the organization and its leaders; its relationship to external world; and its community work. Formal study of either or both organizations would surely yield important new knowledge regarding such challenges and other lessons in the creation and application of effective integral change approaches.

Closing Comments

Integral approaches to change, according to the theoretical framework I have presented throughout this work, are those founded on the integration of liberation and transformation methodologies and on the on-going use of practices that de-

---

[21] Wilber (2000) might likely deem both organizations and their approaches as being at the ethnocentric stage of development, that is, beyond egocentric, but still guided by a fragmented and group-centered worldview, and not yet at the world-centric stage which is guided by an inclusive, transcultural, or integral worldview.

velop skills which, together, support the process of consciousness-in-action toward well-being. Integral change approaches are intended to liberate and transform the practitioner who, in turn, becomes a force and a resource for liberatory-transformative change of others.

In effect, the theoretical framework as presented in its
entirety effectively answers the question posed at the outset:
What would a comprehensive and cohesive conceptual
framework of human well-being in the context of institutional
and internalized oppression look like, one that takes into account multiple perspectives, and that views well-being as a
process of liberation from oppression and development as
transformation at both individual and collective dimensions
of life?

The model of well-being within the sphere of human
activity, as presented in Chapter 2, offers this comprehensive
and cohesive—integral—frame which, when viewed within
the context of the matrix of domination and the dynamics of
oppression (Chapter 3), allows for a multidimensional, multi-
perspectival and historical analysis of human conditions. It is
on the basis of this integral analysis that the processes I have
come to call *consciousness-in-action* (Chapter 4) can be engaged to facilitate growth through the stages of social identity
development. Consciousness-in-action through the developmental stages along multiple lines of social identity (and together with other lines of development, e.g., cognitive, ethi-
cal, emotional, needs, spiritual, worldviews), in turn, enables
processes of liberation and transformation, and integral approaches (Chapter 5) that foster—and demand—individual
involvement and collective leadership in the pursuit of higher
levels of well-being and on-going human development.

This integral framework is comprehensive in nature
as it is built primarily upon three similarly comprehensive or
integrative conceptual and theoretical frameworks: integral
theory (Wilber, 1995), the medicine wheel model (Bopp et

al., 1989), and social identity development theory (Hardiman and Jackson, 1997). As mentioned in the Introduction, the framework also draws from multiple areas within the social sciences and, to a lesser extent, cultural studies, and spirituality. Correspondingly, this framework has implications for scholars and practitioners in many fields, including integral psychology, liberation psychology, community psychology, social psychology, sociology, social theory, social justice education, social work, public policy, and organizational development and transformation, as well as for people engaged in social movement and spiritual activism.[22]

Among the multiple implications the framework could have for these fields, one of the most important revolves around the integral nature of both well-being and the process of liberation and transformation itself. That is, if as agents of change we accept the integral nature of human well-being and development, our analyses of conditions and our approaches to change toward well-being and development will then need to take into account the dynamic, systemic, interdependent, interlocking, and holistic relationships among and between all aspects and all dimensions.

In direct conflict with the fragmented view of dominant culture, this notion of integrality presents challenges at both personal and organizational levels. Groups and organizations adopting an integral approach would need to transcend the usual boundaries of their particular field or ideology; without necessarily giving up their particular perspective of an issue or problem, social change groups would need to look beyond the self- or other-imposed limits of their work. For example, anti-racism organizations, without altering their primary purpose and goals, might consider the impact of other forms of oppression upon their organization and

---

[22] Spiritual activism seeks to integrate spirituality and contemplative practice with social engagement and political activism toward personal liberation and social transformation (Horwitz, 2002).

their change work, and respond to this organizational analysis accordingly. Similarly, groups in Puerto Rico engaged in efforts against US colonialism might also consider liberation and transformation work regarding cultural racism, sexism, homophobia and the entire range of "isms" that also undermine their efforts, while exploring ways to more effectively organize and unite struggles currently separate.

The centrality of integrality to well-being and development, and moreover, to authentic personal power, positive influence, and effective leadership has implications for social change agents at the personal level. The significance of balance (equilibrium) and harmony (congruence) between all aspects and dimensions, and particularly as these principles relate to addressing social group identity dynamics within the matrix of domination, suggests that agents of social change ascribing to an integral liberation-transformation perspective actively seek to resolve emotional and cognitive dissonance between dominant and subordinated aspects with themselves. Such a notion may well set a standard of leadership, both personal and collective, that may appear quite difficult to achieve, thus undermining its adoption as a practical, or even feasible, approach.

Finally, this theoretical framework challenges integral thinkers and practitioners to examine the importance of social identity development to the process of well-being and overall development—especially within the context of the persistent and prevailing reality of oppression throughout the world. Integral psychology and, moreover, integral theory could well add its significant perspective and methodology of transformation were it to address, indeed *integrate*, the need for integral collective liberation.

The integral framework I have presented, hopefully, will contribute to and advance the much needed conversation on liberation and transformation, and stimulate further research and development of context-specific applications across multiple fields of study and action.

Bibliography

Abrams, D., and Michael A. Hogg. (2004). Collective Identity and Self-Conception. In M. B. Brewer and M. Hewstone (Ed.), *Self and Social Identity* (pp. 145-181). Malden, MA: Blackwell Publishing.

Adair, M. (2001). *Meditations on Everything Under the Sun.* Gabriola Island, BC: New Society Publishers.

Adair, M. (2003). *Working Inside Out.* Naperville, Il: Sourcebooks.

Adams, M., Lee Anne Bell, and Pat Griffin (Ed.). (1997). *Teaching for Diversity and Social Justice: A Sourcebook.* New York: Routledge.

Akbar, N. (1984). *Chains and Images of Psychological Slavery.* New Jersey: New Mind Productions.

Akbar, N. (1996). *Breaking the Chains of Psychological Slavery.* Tallahassee, FL: Mind Productions & Associates.

Anderson, S. E. (1995). *The Black Holocaust.* New York: Writers and Readers Publishing.

Ani, M. D. R. (1980). *Let the Circle Be Unbroken: The Implications of African Spirituality in the Diaspora.* New York: Nkonimfo Publications.

Ani, M. D. R. (1994). *Yurugu: An Afrikan-Centered Critique of European Cultural Thought and Behavior.* New Jersey: Africa World Press, Inc.

Arrien, A. (1993). *The Four-Fold Way: Walking the Paths of the Warrior, Teacher, Healer and Visionary.* San Francisco, CA: Harper.

Assagioli, R. (1965/1976). *Psychosynthesis.* New York: Penguin Books.

Assagioli, R. (1973). *The Act of Will.* New York: Penguin Books.

Bandler, R. (1985). *Using Your Brain for a Change.* Moah, Utah: Real People Press.

Bandler, R. (1992a). Design Human Engineering™. San Francisco, CA: The First Institute of Neuro-Linguistic Programming & Design Human Engineering.

Bandler, R. (1992b). *Magic in Action.* Capitola, CA: Meta Publications.

Bandler, R. (1993). *Time for A Change.* Capitola, CA: Meta Publications.

Bandler, R., and Will MacDonald. (1988). *An Insider's Guide to Sub-Modalities.* Capitola, CA: Meta Publications.

Barbalet, J. M. (2001). *Emotion, Social Theory, and Social Structure: A Macrosociological Approach.* Cambridge: Cambridge University Press.

Beck, D. E. (1999). *The Search for Cohesion in the Age of Fragmentation.*

Beck, D. E., and Christopher C. Cowan. (1996). *Spiral Dynamics: Mastering Values, Leadership, and Change.* Malden, MA: Blackwell Publishers.

Bell, L. A. (1997). Theoretical Foundations for Social Justice Education. In M. Adams, Lee Anne Bell, and Pat Griffin (Ed.), *Teaching for Diversity and Social Justice: A Sourcebook.* New York: Routledge.

Berry, J. W., Ype H. Poortinga, Marshall H. Segall, and Pierre R. Dasen (Ed.). (2002). *Cross-Cultural Psychology: Research and Applications*. Cambridge, UK: Cambridge University Press,.

Boal, A. (1985). *Theatre of the Oppressed*. New York: Theatre Communications Group.

Bodenhamer, B. G., and L. Michael Hall. (2000). *The User's Manual for the Brain: the Complete Manual for Neuro-Linguistic Programming Practitioner Certification*. Wales, UK: Crown House Publishing.

Boff, L., and Clodovis Boff. (2004). *Introducing Liberation Theology*. Maryknoll, NY: Orbis Books.

Bopp, J., Michael Bopp, and Phil Lane, Jr. (1998). *Community Healing and Aboriginal Social Security Reform*. Lethbridge, Alberta: The Four Worlds International Institute for Human and Community Development.

Bopp, J., Michael Bopp, Lee Brown, and Phil Lane, Jr. (1984/1989). *The Sacred Tree: Reflections on Native American Spirituality* (Third ed.). Alberta, Canada: Lotus Light Press.

Bopp, M., and Judie Bopp. (2001). *Recreating the World: A Practical Guide to Building Sustainable Communities*. Calgary, Alberta: Four Worlds Press.

Brewer, M. B., and Miles Hewstone (Ed.). (2004). *Self and Social Identity*. Malden, MA: Blackwell Publishing.

Brewer, M. B., and Wendi Gardner. (1996). Who is This "We"? Levels of Collective Identity and Self Representations. *Journal of Personality and Social Psychology, 71*(1), 83-93.

Brown, M. Y. (1983). *The Unfolding Self: Psychosynthesis and Counseling*. Los Angeles, CA: Psychosynthesis Press.

Bulhan, H. A. (1985). *Frantz Fanon and the Psychology of Oppression*. New York: Plenum Press.

Bureau of the Census. (2001). *Profiles of General Demographic Characteristics: 2000 Census of Population and Housing, Puerto Rico.*

Buscaglia-Salgado, J. F. (2003). *Undoing Empire: Race and Nation in the Mulatto Caribbean.* Minneapolis: University of Minnesota Press.

Buzan, T. (1974). *Use Both Sides of Your Brain.* New York: E. P. Dutton.

Bynner, W. (1944). *The Way of Life According to Lao Tzu.* New York: Capricorn Books.

Castaneda, C. (1969). *The Teachings of don Juan: A Yaqui Way of Knowledge.* Berkeley, CA: University of California Press.

Castaneda, C. (1972). *Journey to Ixtlan: The Lessons of don Juan.* New York: Simon and Schuster.

Chisom, R. and Michael Washington. (1997). *Undoing Racism: A Philosophy of International Social Change* (2 ed.). New Orleans, LA: The People's Institute Press.

Collins, D. (1977). *Paulo Freire: His Life, Works & Thought.* New York: Paulist Press.

Comas-Díaz, L. (1996). LatiNegra: Mental Health Issues of African Latinas. In M. P. P. Root (Ed.), *The Multiracial Experience: Racial Borders as the New Frontier* (pp. 167-190). Thousand Oaks: Sage Publications.

Combs, A. (1995/2002). *The Radiance of Being.* St. Paul, Minnesota: Paragon House.

Comisión de Derechos Civiles. (1989). *Discrimen y persecusión por razones políticas: la práctica gubernamental de mantener listas, ficheros y expedientes de ciudadanos por razón de su ideología política.* San Juan: Estado Libre Asociado de Puerto Rico.

Covey, S. R. (1990). *Principle-Centered Leadership.* New York: Summit Books.

Cowan, C. (2005). Premature Integral. *Spiral Dynamics Newsletter*(4).

Cowan, C. C., and Natasha Todorovic. (2000). Spiral Dynamics: The Layers of Human Values in Strategy. 2004, from http://www.spiraldynamics.org/documents

Davis, A. Y. (1998). Political Prisoners, Prisons, and Black Liberation. In J. James (Ed.), *The Angela Y. Davis Reader* (pp. 39-52). Malden, MA: Blackwell Publishers.

Deikman, A. J. (1982). *The Observing Self: Mysticism and Psychotherapy*. Boston: Beacon Press.

Dilts, R. B. (1987). *Healing Patterns of Jesus*.Unpublished manuscript, Capitola, CA.

Dilts, R. B. (1990). *Changing Beliefs Systems with NLP*. Capitola, CA: Meta Publications.

Dilts, R. B. (1996). *Visionary Leadership Skills: Creating a World to Which People Want to Belong*. Capitola, CA: Meta Publications.

Dilts, R. B. (1998). *Modeling with NLP*. Capitola, CA: Meta Publications.

Drury, J., Steve Reicher, and Clifford Stott. (2003). Transforming the Boundaries of Collective Identity: from the "local" anti-road campaign to "global" resistance? *Social Movement Studies, 2*(2), 191-212.

Dussel, E. (1998/2000). *Etica de la liberacion: en la edad de la globalizacion y de la exclusion*. Madrid: Editorial Trotta.

Elgin, D. (1980). The Tao of Personal and Social Transformation. In R. Walsh, and Frances Vaughan (Ed.), *Beyond Ego: Transpersonal Dimensions in Psychology*. Los Angeles: J. P. Tarcher.

Eppsteiner, F. (Ed.). (1988). *The Path of Compassion: Writings on Socially Engaged Buddhism*. Berkeley, CA: Parallax Press.

Fanon, F. (1963). *The Wretched of the Earth*. New York: Grove Weidenfeld.

Fanon, F. (1967). *Black Skin, White Masks.* New York: Grove Press.

Ferdman, B. M., and Plácida I. Gallegos. (2001). Racial Identity Development and Latinos in the United States. In C. L. Wijeyesinghe, and Bailey W. Jackson (Ed.), *New Perspectives on Racial Identity Development: A Theoretical and Practical Approach.* New York: New York University Press.

Ferguson, M. (1980). *The Aquarian Conspiracy: Personal and Social Transformation in the 1980s.* Los Angeles: J. P. Tarcher, Inc.

Ferrer, J. (2003). Integral Transformative Practice: A Participatory Perspective. *Journal of Transpersonal Psychology, 35*(1).

Ferris, S., and Ricardo Sandoval. (1997). *The Fight in the Fields: Cesar Chavez and the Farmworkers Movement.* San Diego: Harcourt Brace & Company.

Ferrucci, P. (1982). *What We May Be.* Los Angeles, CA: J. P. Tarcher.

Firman, J., and Ann Gila. (1997). *The Primal Wound: A Transpersonal View of Trauma, Addiction, and Growth.* Albany, NY: State University of New York Press.

Firman, J., and Ann Gila. (2002). *Psychosynthesis: A Psychology of the Spirit.* Albany, NY: State University of New York Press.

Fisher, D., David Rooke, Bill Torbert (Ed.). (2000). *Personal and Organisational Transformations: Through Action Inquiry* (3rd ed.). Boston, MA: Edge\Work Press.

Fox, D., and Isaac Prilleltensky (Ed.). (1997). *Critical Psychology: An Introduction.* London: Sage Publications.

Frankl, V. E. (1963). *Man's Search for Meaning: An Introduction to Logotherapy.* New York: Washington Square Press.

Freedman, S. G. (1993). *Upon This Rock: The Miracles of a Black Church.* New York: Harper Collins Publishers.

Freire, P. (1970). *Pedagogía del oprimido.* Mexico: Siglo Veitiuno Editores.

Freire, P. (1998). *Pedagogy of Freedom: Ethics, Democracy, and Civic Courage.* Lanham, MD: Rowman & Littlefield.

Freire, P. (2005). *Pedagogy of the Oppressed.* New York: Continuum International.

Gardiner, H. W. and C. Kosmitzki. (2002). *Lives Across Cultures: Cross-Cultural Human Development* (2 ed.). Boston: Allyn and Bacon.

Gilligan, C. (1993). *In a Different Voice: Psychological Theory and Women's Development.* Cambridge, MA: Harvard University Press.

Goenka, S. N. (1987). *The Discourse Summaries.* Seattle, WA: Vipassana Research Publications.

Goleman, D. (1995). *Emotional Intelligence.* New York: Bantam Books.

Graves, C. W. (2002). *Graves: Levels of Human Existence.* Santa Barbara, CA: ECLET Publishing.

Gutierrez, G. (1973/2005). *A Theology of Liberation: History, Politics, and Salvation* (S. C. I . a. J. Eagleson, Trans.). Maryknoll, NY: Orbis Books.

Hall, L. M. (2000). *Meta-States: Mastering the Higher States of Mind.* Clifton, CO: E.T. Publications.

Hall, L. M., Bob G. Bodenhamer, Richard Bolstad, and Margot Hamblett. (2001). *The Structure of Personality: Modeling "Personality" Using NLP and Neuro-Semantics.* Wales, UK: Crown House Publishing Limited.

Hardiman, R., and Bailey W. Jackson. (1997). Conceptual Foundations for Social Justice Courses. In M. Adams, Lee Anne Bell, and Pat Griffin (Ed.), *Teaching for Diversity and Social Justice.* New York: Routledge.

Hart, W. (1987). *The Art of Living: Vipassana Meditation as Taught by S. N. Goenka*. New York, NY: Harper-Collins Publishers.

Herman, J. (1992). *Trauma and Recovery*. New York: Basic Books.

Hill Collins, P. (1990). Black Feminist Thought in the Matrix of Domination. In C. Lemert (Ed.), *Social Theory: The Multicultural and Classic Readings*. Boulder, CO: Westview Press.

Hill Collins, P. (2000). *Black Feminist Thought: Knowledge, Consciousness, and the Politics of Empowerment* (2nd Edition ed.). New York: Routledge.

Hollander, N. C. (1997). *Love in a Time of Hate: Liberation Psychology in Latin America*. New Brunswick, NJ: Rutgers University Press.

hooks, b. (1993). *Sisters of the Yam: Black Women and Self-Recovery*. Boston: South End Press.

hooks, b. (1995). *Killing Rage: Ending Racism*. New York: Henry Holt and Company.

hooks, b. (2000a). *Feminism is for Everybody: Passionate Politics*. Boston: South End Press.

hooks, b. (2000b). *Feminist Theory: From Margin to Center* (2nd ed.). Boston: South End Press.

Hope, A., and Sally Timmel. (1984). *Training for Transformation: A Handbook for Community Workers* (Vol. 1). Gweru, Zimbabwe: Mambo Press.

Hope, A., and Sally Timmel. (1999). *Training for Transformation: A Handbook for Community Workers* (Vol. 4). London: ITDG Publishing.

Horton, M., and Paulo Freire. (1990). *We Make the Road by Walking: Conversations on Education and Social Change*. Philadelphia: Temple University Press.

Horwitz, C. (2002). *The Spiritual Activist: Practices to Transform Your Life, Your Work, and Your World*. New York: Penguin Compass.

Houston, J. (1982). *The Possible Human.* Los Angeles, CA: Jeremy P. Tarcher, Inc.

Houston, J. (2000). *Jump Time: Shaping Your Future in a World of Radical Change.* New York: Tarcher/Putnam.

Hurtado, A. (1996). *The Color of Privilege: Three Blasphemies on Race and Feminism.* Ann Arbor, MI: University of Michigan Press.

Ignatiev, N. (1995). *How The Irish Became White.* New York: Routledge.

Jackson, B. W. (2001). Black Identity Development: Further Analysis and Elaboration. In C. L. Wijeyesinghe and B. W. Jackson III (Ed.), *New Perspectives on Racial Identity Development: A Theoretical and Practical Anthology.* New York: New York University Press.

Jacobs, J. E., Martha M. Bleeker, and Michael J. Constantino. (2003). The Self-System During Childhood and Adolescence: Development, Influences, and Implications. *Journal of Psychotherapy Integration, 13*(1), 33-65.

James, J. (Ed.). (1998). *The Angela Y. Davis Reader.* Malden, MA: Blackwell Publishers.

Jung, C. G. (1968). *Man and His Symbols.* New York: Dell Publishing.

Kapleau, P. (1980). *The Three Pillars of Zen.* Garden City, NY: Anchor Press/Doubleday.

Kegan, R. (1982). *The Evolving Self: Problem and Process in Human Development.* Cambridge. MA: Harvard University Press.

Kiecolt, K. J. (2000). Self-Change in Social Movement. In S. Stryker, T. J. Owens, and R. W. White (Ed.), *Self, Identity, and Social Movements.* Minneapolis, MS: University of Minnesota Press.

Kokopeli, B., and George Lakey. (1978). *Leadership for Change: Toward a Feminist Model.* Santa Cruz, CA: New Society Publishers.

Lankton, S. R. (1980). *Practical Magic: A Translation of Basic Neuro-Linguistic Programming into Clinical Psychotherapy.* Capitola, CA: Meta Publications.

Leary, J. D. (2005). *Post Traumatic Slave Syndrome: America's Legacy of Enduring Injury and Healing.* Milwaukie, OR: Uptone Press.

Leonard, G., and Michael Murphy. (1995). *The Life We are Given.* New York: Jeremy P. Tarcher/Putnam.

Leondar-Wright, B. (2005). *Class Matters.* Gabriola Island, BC: New Society Publishers.

Lester, J., and Carol Johnson. (1990). *Training of Trainers Intensive Program Manual.* Unpublished manuscript, Amherst, MA.

Levins Morales, A. (1998). *Medicine Stories: History, Culture and the Politics of Integrity.* Cambridge, MA: South End Press.

Levins Morales, A. (2001). Certified Organic Intellectual. In Latina Feminist Group (Ed.), *Telling to Live: Latina Feminist Testimonios* (pp. 27-32). Durham: Duke University Press.

Loevinger, J. (1976). *Ego Development: Conceptions and Theories.* San Francisco: Jossey-Bass, Inc., Publishers.

Lörler, M.-L. (1991). *Shamanic Healing within the Medicine Wheel.* Albuquerque, NM: Brotherhood of Life.

Martín-Baró, I. (1989). *Sistema, grupo y poder: Psicología social desde Centroamérica II.* San Salvador: UCA Editores.

Martín-Baró, I. (1994). *Writings for a Liberation Psychology.* Cambridge, MA: Harvard University Press.

Martinez, E. (Ed.). (1991). *500 Years of Chicano History in Pictures.* Albuquerque, NM: SouthWest Organizing Project.

Marx, K., and Friedrich Engels. (1888/2002). *The Communist Manifesto* (S. Moore, Trans.). London: Penguin Books.

Maslow, A. H. (1968). *Toward a Psychology of Being* (2nd ed.). New York: Van Nostrand Reinhold.

Maslow, A. H. (1971). *The Farther Reaches of Human Nature*. New York: Penguin Books.

May, R. (1953). *Man's Search for Himself*. New York: Dell Publishing.

McLaren, P., and Peter Leonard (Ed.). (1993). *Paulo Freire: A Critical Encounter*. London: Routledge.

McManus, P., and Gerald Schlabach (Ed.). (1991). *Relentless Persistence: Non-Violent Action in Latin America*. Philadelphia: New Society Publishers.

Merlevede, P. E., Denis Bridoux, and Rudy Vandamme. (2001). *7 Steps to Emotional Intelligence*. Wales, UK: Crown House Publishing Limited.

Meyerhoff, J. (2005). Bald Ambition: A Critique of Ken Wilber's Theory of Everything [Electronic Version]. http://www.integralworld.net/index.html?visser12.html.

Meyerhoff, J. (2006). Six Criticisms of Wilber's Integral Theory [Electronic Version]. *Integral World* from http://www.integralworld.net/index.html?visser12.html.

Moane, G. (1999). *Gender and Colonialism: A Psychological Analysis of Oppression and Liberation*. New York: St. Martin's Press.

Moane, G. (2003). Bridging the Personal and the Political: Practices for a Liberation Psychology. *American Journal of Community Psychology, 31*(1/2), 91-102.

Moane, G. (2006). Exploring Activism and Change: Feminist Psychology, Liberation Psychology, Political Psychology. *Feminism & Psychology, 16*(1), 73-78.

Mohanty, C. T. (2003). *Feminism Without Borders: Decolo-nizing Theory, Practicing Solidarity.* Durham: Duke University Press.

Montero, M. (1994). *Construcción y crítica de la psicología social.* Barcelona, Spain, and Caracas, Venezuela: Editorial Anthropos.

Montero, M. (1997). *Ideología, alienación e identidad nacional.* Caracas, Venezuela: Ediciones de la Biblioteca, Universidad Central de Venezuela.

Montero, M. (2003). *Teoria y practica de la psicologia comunitaria: la tension entre comunidad y sociedad.* Buenos Aires, Argentina: Paidos.

Montero, M. (2004). *Introduccion a la psicologia comunitaria: Desarrollo, conceptos y procesos.* Buenos Aires, Argentina: Paidos.

Montero, M. (Ed.). (1987). *Psicología política latinoamericana.* Caracas, Venezuela: Editorial Panapo.

Montero, M. (Ed.). (1991). *Acción y discurso: Problemática de psicología política en América Latina.* Venezuela: Eduven.

Moreno Vega, M. (2000). *The Altar of My Soul: The Living Traditions of Santería.* New York: One World/Ballantine Books/Random House.

Nelson, G., and Issac Prilleltensky (Ed.). (2005). *Community Psychology: In Pursuit of Liberation and Well-Being.* New York: Palgrave Macmillan.

Nhat Hanh, T. (1992). *Touching Peace: Practicing the Art of Mindful Living.* Berkeley, CA: Parrallax Press.

O'Connor, J. (1998). *Leading with NLP: Essential Leadership Skills for Influencing and Managing People.* London: Thorsons/HarperCollins Publishers.

Ouspensky, P. D. (1957). *The Fourth Way.* New York: Vintage.

Perls, F. (1975). *The Gestalt Approach & Eye Witness to Therapy.* New York: Bantam.

Pinker, S. (2002). *The Blank Slate: The Modern Denial of Human Nature*. New York: Viking.

Prilleltensky, I. (2003). Understanding, Resisting, and Overcoming Oppression: Toward Psychopolitical Validity. *American Journal of Community Psychology, 31*(1/2), 195.

Prilleltensky, I., and Geoffrey Nelson. (1997). Community Psychology: Reclaiming Social Justice. In D. Fox, and Isaac Prilleltensky (Ed.), *Critical Psychology: An Introduction*. London: Sage Publications.

Quijano, A. (2000). Colonialidad del poder y clasificacion social. *Journal of World-Systems Research, XI*(2), 342-386.

Quiñones Rosado, R. (1989). *The Emergence of Holism in Corporate America*. Unpublished Masters, Cambridge College, Northampton, MA.

Quiñones Rosado, R. (1998). Hispanic or Latino? The Struggle for Identity in a Race-Based Society. *The Diversity Factor, 6*(4).

Quiñones Rosado, R., and Esterla Barreto-Cortéz. (2000). Un modelo de bienestar integral y sus implicaciones a la práctica de profesionales de ayuda. *Análisis, Escuela Graduada de Trabajo Social, Universidad de Puerto Rico, Río Piedras, PR, 2*(1).

Quiñones Rosado, R., and Esterla Barreto-Cortéz. (2002). An Integral Model of Well-Being and Development and Its Implications for Helping Professions. *Journal of Human Behavior in the Social Environment, 5*(3/4).

Quiñones-Rosado, R., and Esterla Barreto-Cortéz. (2002). An Integral Model of Well-Being and Development and Its Implications for Helping Professions. In J. B. Torres and F. G. Rivera (Ed.), *Latino/Hispanic Liaisons and Visions for Human Behavior in the Social Environment*. New York: The Haworth Social Work Practice Press.

Rappaport, J. (1981). In Praise of Paradox: A Social Policy of Empowerment over Prevention. *American Journal of Community Psychology, 9*, 1-25.

Reinat Pumarejo, M. I. (2005). Conquistas que matan: Imposición racial en Puerto Rico. *Plaza Crítica, 2.*

Rivera Ramos, E. (2001). *The Legal Construction of Identity: The Judicial and Social Legacy of American Colonialism in Puerto Rico.* Washington, DC: American Psychological Association.

Roberson, E. D. (1995). *The Maafa & Beyond: Remembrance, Ancestral Connections and Nation Building for the African Global Community.* Columbia, MD: Kujichagulia Press.

Rodríguez, C. E. (2000). *Changing Race: Latinos, the Census, and the History of Ethnicity in the United States.* New York: New York University Press.

Rogers, C. (1961). *On Becoming a Person: A Therapist's View of Psychotherapy.* Boston: Houghton Mifflin Company.

Root, M. P. P. (1992). Reconstructing the Impact of Trauma on Personality. In L. S. Brown, and Mary Ballou (Ed.), *Personality and Psychopathology: Feminist Reappraisals* (pp. 229-265). New York: The Guilford Press.

Rose, C. (1985). *Accelerated Learning.* New York: Dell Publishing.

Saldaña Portillo, M. J. (2002). Reading a Silence: The "Indian" of the Era of Zapatismo. *Nepantla: Views from South, 3*(2), 287-314.

Sandoval, C. (2000). *Methodology of the Oppressed.* Minneapolis, MN: University of Minnesota Press.

Scharmer, C. O. (2004). The View from 50,000 Feet: An Integral Approach to Presencing. Retrieved March 3, 2004.

Serrano-Garcia, I., and Nelson Varas-Diaz. (2003). The Challenge to a Positive Self-Image in a Colonial Context: A Psychology of Liberation for the Puerto Rican Experience. *American Journal of Community Psychology, 31*(1/2), 103-115.

Serrano-Garcia, I., and Roderick J. Watts. (2003). The Quest for a Liberating Community Psychology: An Overview. *American Journal of Community Psychology, 31*(1/2), 73-78.

Shor, I. (1992). *Empowering Education: Critical Teaching for Social Change.* Chicago: University of Chicago Press.

Sidanius, J., and Felicia Pratto. (1999). *Social Dominance: An Intergroup Theory of Social Hierarchy and Oppression.* New York: Cambridge University Press.

Sivaraksa, S. (1992). *Seeds of Peace: A Buddhist Vision for Renewing Society.* Berkeley, CA: Parallax Press.

Smith, L. T. (1999). *Decolonizing Methodologies: Research and Indigenous Peoples.* New York: Zed Books, Ltd.

Stanfield, R. B. (2000). *The Courage to Lead: Transform Self, Transform Society.* Gabriola Island BD, Canada: New Society Publishers.

Stryker, S., and Timothy J. Owens, and Robert W. White (Ed.). (2000). *Self, Identity, and Social Movements* (Vol. 13). Minneapolis: University of Minnesota Press.

Suro, R., Mollyann Brodie, Annie Steffenson, Jaime Valdez, and Rebecca Levin. (2002). *2002 National Survey of Latinos* (Summary of Findings). Washington, DC: Pew Hispanic Center / Kaiser Family Foundation.

Suzuki, D. T. (1973). *An Introduction to Zen Buddhism.* New York: Ballantine Books.

Szasz, T. S. (1960). The Myth of Mental Illness. *American Psychologist, 15,* 113-118.

Tart, C. T. (1992). *Transpersonal Psychologies: Perspectives on the Mind from Seven Great Spiritual Traditions.* New York: Harper Collins.

Tatum, B. D. (1997). *"Why Are All the Black Kids Sitting Together in the Cafeteria?" and Other Conversations About Race.* New York: Basic Books.

Vaughn, F. (2003). Psychotherapy and Meditation. *Internal Naked* Retrieved 4/26/2004, from www.integralnaked.org

Visser, F. (2006a). Games Pandits Play: A Reply to Ken Wilber's Raging Rant [Electronic Version] from http://www.integralworld.net/index.html?visser12.html.

Visser, F. (2006b). Talking Back to Wilber: A Call for Validation [Electronic Version]. *Integral World* from http://www.integralworld.net/.

Vygotsky, L. S. (1978). *Mind in Society: the Development of Higher Psychological Processes.* Cambridge, MA: Harvard University Press.

Wade, J. (1996). *Changes of Mind: A Holonomic Theory of the Evolution of Consciousness.* Albany, NY: State University of New York Press.

Walsh, R. (1984). *Staying Alive: The Psychology of Human Survival.* Boulder, CO: New Science Library/Shambhala.

Walsh, R. (1999). *Essential Spirituality: The 7 Central Practices to Awaken Heart and Mind.* New York: John Wiley & Sons.

Walsh, R., and Frances Vaughn (Ed.). (1980). *Beyond Ego: Transpersonal Dimensions in Psychology.* Los Angeles, CA: J. P. Tarcher, Inc.

Watts, R. J., Nat Chioke Williams, and Robert J. Jagers. (2003). Sociopolitical Development. *American Journal of Community Psychology, 31*(1/2), 185-194.

Welwood, J. (2000). *Toward a Psychology of Awakening: Buddhism, Psychotherapy, and the Path of Personal and Spiritual Transformation.* Boston: Shambhala.

Wijeyesinghe, C. L., and Bailey W. Jackson (Ed.). (2001). *New Perspectives on Racial Identity Development: A Theoretical and Practical Anthology.* New York: New York University Press.

Wilber, K. (1977). *The Spectrum of Consciousness.* Wheaton, IL: The Theosophical Publishing House.

Wilber, K. (1980). *The Atman Project: A Transpersonal View of Human Development.* Wheaton, IL: The Theosophical Publishing House.

Wilber, K. (1981). *Up From Eden: A Transpersonal View of Human Evolution.* New York: Anchor Press/Doubleday.

Wilber, K. (1996). *A Brief History of Everything.* Boston: Shambhala.

Wilber, K. (1997). *The Eye of Spirit: An Integral Vision for a World Gone Slightly Mad.* Boston: Shambhala.

Wilber, K. (1998). *The Marriage of Sense and Soul: Integrating Science and Religion.* New York: Random House.

Wilber, K. (1999a). Integral Psychology. In *The Collected Works of Ken Wilber* (Vol. 4). Boston: Shambhala.

Wilber, K. (1999b). *One Taste: The Journals of Ken Wilber.* Boston: Shambhala.

Wilber, K. (1999c). Sociocultural Evolution. In *The Collected Works of Ken Wilber* (Vol. 4). Boston: Shambhala.

Wilber, K. (1999d). Transformations of Consciousness. In *The Collected Works of Ken Wilber* (Vol. 4). Boston: Shambhala.

Wilber, K. (2000a). *A Theory of Everything: An Integral Vision for Business, Politics, Science, and Spirituality.* Boston: Shambhala.

Wilber, K. (2000b). Outline of An Integral Psychology. Retrieved in 2002, from www.shambhala.com

Wilber, K. (2000d). *Sex, Ecology, Spirituality: The Spirit of Evolution* (2 ed.). Boston: Shambhala.

Wilber, K. (2002). *Boomeritis: A Novel that Will Set You Free*. Boston: Shambhala.

Wilber, K. (2003a). *Introduction to Integral Theory and Practice: IOS Basic and the AQAL Map*. Unpublished manuscript, Boulder, CO.

Wilber, K. (2003b). The Integral Approach. Retrieved in 2003, from www.shambhala.com

Wineman, S. (2003). *Power-Under: Trauma and Non-Violent Social Change*. Unpublished manuscript, Cambridge, MA.

Worchel, S., and Dawna Coutant. (2004). It Takes Two to Tango: Relating Group Identity to Individual Identity within the Frameworks of Group Development. In M. B. Brewer and M. Hewstone (Ed.), *Self and Social Identity* (pp. 182-202). Malden, MA: Blackwell Publishing.

Zinn, H. (1995). *A People's History of the United States: 1492 to Present*. New York: HarperCollins.

Appendix

Hardiman & Jackson's Social Identity Development Model

Stage	Agents (Dominant)	Targets (Subordinated)
Naïve Between birth and ages 3-4, agents and targets alike...	Have **no social consciousness**; are **unaware of differences** between social identity groups, and of the complex social codes and dynamics of these groups. **Learn** about their social identities as they violate boundaries of their social group(s).	
As children exit the naïve stage, they...	Begin to **internalize** belief systems about their own and other's social group identities. Also **socialized** regarding *power*, they learn about rules, laws, institutions, authority figures that allow (and reward) certain behaviors and prohibit (and punish) others, and how these apply differentially to different people depending on their social identity group.	

Acceptance	Passive	Active	Passive	Active
Generally from childhood through adulthood. Entry into this stage represents some degree of...	1) **Unconscious internalization** of and **identification** with dominant culture's logic, values, feelings and beliefs and codes of appropriate behavior. **Covertly taught** about the alleged inferiority of targeted people.	1) **Conscious internalization** of and **identification** with the dominant culture which give them privilege as a members of an agent group. **Overtly taught** about the alleged inferiority of targeted people.	1) **Unconscious internalization** and **acceptance of** dominant culture's logic, values, feelings and beliefs systems and codes of appropriate behavior: inferiority of their group; superiority of dominant group.	1) **Conscious identification** and **acceptance** of dominant culture's logic, values, feelings and beliefs systems and codes of appropriate behavior: inferiority of their group; superiority of dominant group.
Acceptance (cont...)	2) **Unaware** of their status as dominant group members; privileges perceived as normative. **Deny** the existence of oppression. **Blame** the oppressed for their condition; paternalistically agree to help them overcome their self-made condition so that they will fit into the dominant group's system.	2) **Believe** in the superiority of own group, and tend to promote these beliefs more directly. **Blame** oppressed people for their condition and actively propagate negative stereotypes. **Reward** those who support the oppressive system, and **punish** those who question or challenge the system.	2) **Deny** the existence of oppression, and unwittingly **collude** with the oppressive system.	2) **Rationalize** their acquiescence to and/or active support of the oppressive culture and system. **Ignore** contradictions inherent in the rationalization of their active participation in their own oppression.
Life experiences that challenge this worldview lead them to **exit** this phase, as they begin to...	3) **Acknowledge** existence of some injustices in society; that the oppressed group's condition may not be all their doing.	3) **Acknowledge** existence of some injustices in the society; that the oppresses group's condition may not be all their own doing.	3) **Acknowledge** existence of some overt forms of oppression; begin to see these as more than just occasional exceptions.	3) **Acknowledge** contradictions, and dissonance between dominant ideology and the positive attributes of own group.

Resistance	Passive	Active	Passive	Active
Entry into this stage comes with increased awareness of oppression and its impacts, as they...	1) **Search** for examples of oppression in the behavior of individuals and institutions. **Question and challenge** oppression in safe situations where there is little or no risk to social and professional position.	1) **Question** and **examine** the social dynamics and structures that support oppression. Challenge oppression whenever it is identified in people and institutions.	1) **Question and challenge** oppression in safe situations where there is little or no risk to social and professional position.	1) Openly question individual and institutional support for oppressive practices and policies. Seek to gain increased understanding of the nature of oppression; become more skilled at identifying the many ways that it manifests.
	2) **Recognize** the existence of oppression and its pervasiveness throughout society. This often results in their attempt to **distance** themselves from members of their own dominant group.	2) **Feel** shame and guilt at the existence of oppression, and **anger** at other of their own social group. **Take ownership** of own oppressive behavior and their implicit support of oppressive institutions.	2) Experience feelings of **frustration, pain and anger**. Continue to take greater risks through more open challenges of oppression.	2) Increased **anger, pain, hurt & rage** regarding their oppression. Become more hostile toward agents and targets who collude with oppression. Identity defined in **opposition** to oppressor; tries to **cleanse** self of beliefs, attitudes and behaviors learned at Acceptance.
Exit from this stage involves intense feelings and the urge to address questions about their identity, as they...	3) **Feel alienation** and **frustration,** often leading to more actively engage problem. Begin to own their own participation in the oppressive system, and reject its tenets.	3) **Actively reject** own oppressive behavior, attitudes, and privilege, and social system that teaches and supports oppression.	3) Feel an increasing **sense of power** with each direct challenge of oppression.	3) Realize a **sense of power** related to an ability to influence the immediate environment. Develop a clearer sense of "who I am <u>not</u>".

Redefinition Entry is characterized by <u>conscious</u> efforts to create identities independent of the oppressive system. Therefore, people…	1) **Search** for new ways of defining their social group and their membership in it in ways other than based on oppression and stereotyping of target groups.	1) **Focus** attention more on their own social group; do not tend to associate much with agents, as they do not perceive these as being affirming of their new and positive identity.
	2) **Critically examine** their own socialization with other members of the same social group. Recognize differences between social groups, but without attributing superiority or inferiority to any.	2) **Search** to rename [and reframe] their experience and basic referents through new and affirming paradigms; tend to interact more with others at the same developmental stage within their own group.
Exit from this stage begins as people…	3) **Develop** positive definition of their social identity as they discover aspects of their culture they find to be affirming. Develop new sense of pride and personal esteem, and act more spontaneously on their values.	3) **Reclaim** their group's culture; rediscover positive aspects of their heritage, and develop a renewed appreciation and sense of pride in their group identity.

Internalization	1) **Integrate** the new identity into all the various aspects of their life.	1) **Integrate** the new identity into all the various aspects of their life. Continue to internalized new sense of group pride.
Entry occurs as persons begins to associate into their redefined identity, and…		
	2) New identity is **internalized**, and largely unconscious, as they become more comfortable with the application of their new consciousness in everyday life.	2) Expand circle of social interaction beyond supportive reference group; expand circle of influence. Renegotiate important relationships based on new consciousness.
On-going process of refining identity…	3) New identity must be **nurtured** in order for it may be sustained in a hostile environment and against new and improved attempts to resocialize it in the ideology of the oppressive society.	3) Gain a better understanding of the different forms of oppression; appreciation of other target groups; better understanding of the inter-relatedness of oppressions. More capable of transferring growth to other identities.

Sources:

Jackson, Bailey W., and Rita Hardiman. <u>Conceptual Foundations for Social Justice Courses</u>, *Teaching For Diversity and Social Justice*, M. Adams, L.A. Bell & P. Griffin, eds., Routledge, New York. 1997.

Jackson, Bailey W. <u>Black Identity Development: Further Analysis and Elaboration</u>, *New Perspectives on Racial Identity Development: A Theoretical and Practical Anthology*, C. L. Wijeyesinghe and B. W. Jackson III, eds., New York University Press, NY, 2001.

About the Author

Raúl Quiñones-Rosado, PhD, works within various communities-of-struggle in Puerto Rico and the United States to support the on-going development of people committed to personal change and social transformation.

He is co-founder and former co-director of ilé, inc. (previously known as the Institute for Latino Empowerment), an organization committed to anti-oppression community organizing and Latino leadership development. Currently, Raúl directs ilé: c-Integral, a core service of ilé, through which he teaches, counsels, and trains others in the principles and practices of *consciousness-in-action* or integral liberatory transformation.

Raúl began his community work in the US in a variety of social service settings from the early 1970s through the mid-1980s. Later, as executive director of Casa Latina, Inc., a Latino community organization in western Massachusetts, he developed numerous innovative Latino-centered programs. Since 1990, Raúl has been designing and organizing anti-oppression strategies in the US and in Puerto Rico, providing leadership development in community and organizational settings.

As a community organizer, psycho-educational counselor, and social theorist, Raúl has a special interest in the development of integral approaches to liberation and transformation and the healing of internalized oppression.

His published works include:

- An Integral Model of Well-Being and Development and its Implications for Helping Professions. Co-authored with Esterla Barreto Cortez, PhD, *Latino/Hispanic Liaisons and Visions for Human Behavior in the Social Environment*, José B. Torres, and Felix G. Rivera, Eds., The Haworth Social Work Practice Press, New York. 2002.
- Toward an Integral Strategy for Change and Transformation. *Planners Network*, No. 152, Planners Network, Inc., New York. Summer 2002.
- Hispanic or Latino? The Struggle for Identity in a Race-Based Society. *The Diversity Factor*, Vol. 6, No. 4. Elsie Y. Cross Publications, Philadelphia, PA. 1998.
- *Toward an Integral Psychology of Liberation & Transformation*. Doctoral dissertation, Union Institute & University, UMI. 2007.

Raúl lives in Puerto Rico with his partner, María I. Reinat-Pumarejo, and their son, Gabriel Hatuey.

About ilé

ilé, formerly *Institute for Latino Empowerment,* is dedicated to community organizing and leadership development in the United States and Puerto Rico. We work toward creating personal, community, institutional, and systemic changes that lead to liberation from racism, classism, sexism, militarism, and other forms of oppression, and that foster social transformation.

Our goals are: (1) to develop, support, and strengthen the leadership of Latinos/as who struggle against oppression in their communities; (2) to promote integral community organizing as a key process for collective development and self-determination within Latino communities, and; (3) to facilitate effective collaborations, both among Latinas/os, and between Latinos and African Americans, Native Americans, Asian Americans, whites, and others also committed to anti-racist social transformation.

Through all of our efforts, we seek to organize and help people move toward *consciousness-in-action.* We do this work at home in Puerto Rico, with people in Latino communities in the United States, and with groups internationally. Our work has benefited thousands of people since ilé's founding in 1992.

Anti-racism organizing in the US

ilé: Organizers for Consciousness-in-Action does much of its anti-racism organizing in the US through its workshops, *Pa'lante Unidos: Latinos Organizing Against Racism* (for Latino/a audiences) and *Don't be eRACEd by the Census* (for racially mixed audiences). Participants engage in a critical analysis of power and the destructive impact of racism upon Latino communities. Both workshops focus on current efforts in the US to rapidly assimilate light-skinned Latinas/os into the white collective, which undermine not only our cultural and political identities, but weaken the movement against racism. In these workshops, as in our presentations and other organizing activities, we also address: the Census and the changing demographics; national and cultural identity, and the "Hispanic or Latino" debate; colorism, privilege, and cross-group hostility; internalized oppression; and the healing power of culture; response-able leadership, integrity and accountability; organizing among Latinos/as; multi-racial alliance-building; visioning and planning.

Community organizing in Puerto Rico

Avoiding issue-reactive and fragmented approaches to social problems, we organize against racism, sexism, classism, militarism, and colonialism here at home. Our community organizing training program prepares and supports local organizers in dealing with the complexities of integral anti-oppression organizing. Sessions provide foundational knowledge and skills training, while engaging organizers in critical analysis of the matrix of domination and the cyclone of oppression, and ever deeper insight into specific issues confronted in their work. Group and individual work to address and counter internalized oppression is central to the program.

Cultural organizing is a strategy central to ilé's vision of social transformation. Projects like *África en mi piel, África en mi ser* ("Africa on my Skin, Africa in my Soul"), the *Hilvanando visions de paz* quilt, *Alzan su voz* children's speak out for peace, and the use of popular theater allow community members to directly explore, express and experience the healing power of culture.

International organizing and networking

We frequently gather and actively collaborate with other activists and organizers in Puerto Rico and around the globe. Our associations with groups, such as *East Asia-US-Puerto Rico Women's Network Against Militarism, Peace-Watch/Ireland*, and *The People's Institute*, help us connect and share with people in struggle in Okinawa, Japan, the Philippines, South Korea, South Africa, Northern Ireland, and the United States.

Personal and leadership coaching

Through *ilé: c-Integral*, we provide psycho-educational counseling and leadership coaching to help community change workers address issues that may be hindering their personal well-being as well as their leadership and organizing effectiveness. Presentations, workshops and courses on c-Integral's unique socio-psycho-spiritual approach are also available.

Organizational development consultation

ilé also works with community groups and organizations on program planning, organizational development issues, and with other transformative processes from an anti-oppression perspective.

News, information and knowledge products

We keep people in our networks informed about each other's struggles through regular communications. We also share insights, approaches, and original materials on oppression, transformation, and the process of integral change through our website, our weblog, and through our newest social enterprise: *ilé Publications*.

For more information, please contact:

ilé, inc.
ile@conciencia-en-accion.org
www.conciencia-en-accion.org
blog.conciencia-en-accion.org

ilé: c-Integral
raulqr@c-integral.com
www.c-integral.com